100
BEST-SELLING
ALBUMS OF THE
70s

100 BEST-SELLING ALBUMS OF THE 70s

Hamish Champ

THUNDER BAY
P·R·E·S·S

San Diego, California

Thunder Bay Press
An imprint of Printers Row Publishing Group
10350 Barnes Canyon Road, Suite 100, San Diego, CA 92121
www.thunderbaybooks.com

All other correspondence (author inquiries, permissions) concerning the content of this book should be addressed to
Amber Books, United House, North Road, London, N7 9DP, United Kingdom
www.amberbooks.co.uk
Project Editor: Tom Broder
Design: Colin Hawes
Picture Research: Natasha Jones
Consultant: Roger Watson

Thunder Bay Press
Publisher: Peter Norton
Associate Publisher: Ana Parker
Publishing/Editorial Team: April Farr, Kelly Larsen, Kathryn C. Dalby
Editorial Team: JoAnn Padgett, Melinda Allman, Dan Mansfield

Library of Congress Cataloging-in-Publication Data

Names: Champ, Hamish, author.
Title: 100 best-selling albums of the 70s / Hamish Champ.
Description: San Diego, CA : Thunder Bay Press, 2018. | Includes bibliographical references and index.
Identifiers: LCCN 2017055448 | ISBN 9781684123636 (paper over board : alk. paper)
Subjects: LCSH: Popular music--1971-1980--Discography.
Classification: LCC ML156.4.P6 C43 2018 | DDC 016.78164026/6--dc23
LC record available at https://lccn.loc.gov/2017055448

Printed in China

22 21 20 19 18   2 3 4 5 6

Contents

Editor's Foreword

The ranking of the 100 best-selling albums of the 1970s listed in the following pages is based upon US and UK figures: the number of platinum and multi-platinum sales as certified by the Recording Industry Association of America (RIAA), the silver, gold, and platinum sales as certified by the British Phonographic Industry (BPI), as well as figures supplied by the UK's Official Chart Company.

In an industry not always noted for the accuracy of its published sales figures, these awards provide one of the most effective and reliable ways to measure sales success. The figures represent minimum sales for each album, but they do provide a consistent way to rate the relative position of the decade's best-sellers.

These figures also have the advantage—unlike similar lists based on chart position—of showing album sales from the date of first release right up to the present day, meaning that the success of an album such as Pink Floyd's *Dark Side of the Moon*, which has sold consistently well in each decade since its release in 1973, is properly reflected in its position.

Compilation or greatest hits albums are not included in this list, although live albums and original soundtracks, where all of the songs have been collected together or recorded specifically for the album, are included.

Ranking of equal sellers

Where two or more albums have the same sales total they are arranged by date of release, with the most recent album released ranked highest, since its sales are stronger relative to time spent on the market. The Carpenters' *A Song For You* (1972), for example, has had more than six years longer to achieve its three platinum awards than The Doobie Brothers' 1978 release *Minute by Minute*, and is therefore ranked lower in the list.

US and UK album sales

Given the sheer size of the album market in the USA relative to the UK, it is no surprise that US acts dominate across the Top 100. And yet it is UK acts—Led Zeppelin, Pink Floyd, and the Bee Gees—that feature more heavily in the Top Ten.

Also, some UK acts rank here even though they made little impression on the US charts. For example, Mike Oldfield's *Tubular Bells* has sold more than 2,700,000 copies in the UK—more than five times what it has in the US—pushing it to Number 73 in the combined charts. Similarly, *Jeff Wayne's Musical Version of the War of the Worlds* didn't reach platinum status in the US, but UK sales have been strong enough to make it rank at Number 95.

Facts and figures

The appendices provide a breakdown of some of the most interesting facts and figures found throughout this book. You can find out which artists have the most albums in the list and who are the highest-ranking US and UK acts. You can see which albums have won the most Grammy Awards or contain the most Number One singles, what were the best-selling soundtracks and live albums, and which record labels were the most successful of the decade.

Alongside tributes to old favorites, there are enough surprises to keep the most dedicated music buff guessing and stimulate plenty of lively discussion. The iconic 1976 release by Led Zeppelin, *The Song Remains the Same*, for example, was outsold by Kenny Rogers' now often-neglected album *The Gambler*.

The albums featured here are illustrated using a mixture of the US and UK sleeve designs—a selection that includes some of the most arresting graphic design in a decade noted for its album artworks.

The Bee Gees' soundtrack to the 1977 movie *Saturday Night Fever* contains four tracks that went on to become Number One singles— more than any other record among the 100 best-selling albums.

The Best-selling Albums of the 1970s

Describing the 1970s to journalists in early 1980 as "a drag," ex-Beatle John Lennon was noting that the world had become a more dangerous place, with news of war and unrest hitting the headlines on an all-too-regular basis. In popular culture, too, the hippie ideals of the 1960s had been swept away by punk and new wave, replaced by an edgier, more selfish outlook.

In terms of the range and variety of music, however, the decade to which Lennon referred was anything but a drag. The 1970s were a boom period on both sides of the Atlantic, both for the creative output of artists and musicians and for the fortunes of the music industry itself. Record sales, both albums and singles, were growing beyond executives' wildest forecasts. More music was being made available than ever before; newer styles and fresher, more innovative sounds were coming to the fore. Punk, new wave, progressive rock, soul, reggae, dance, disco; they all either burst onto the scene for the first time in the 1970s or, if already established, were developed, enhanced, and improved.

It was a time when older acts could still sell lots of records and make their mark on the charts. Elvis Presley, for example, saw his career take a significant turn for the better. His 1973 album *Aloha From Hawaii* scored his first US Number One long-playing record since 1965. The Rolling Stones went on rolling. The Beatles, too, managed a last-gasp showing in 1970 with *Let It Be*, their final release as a band.

Meanwhile, expectations for the new decade, socially, politically, and culturally, were high. It was an innovative time, an age of space travel and technological advance. Change was in the air.

The legacy of the 1960s

Having seen the ideals of the "peace and love" era amount to little, people approached the 1970s hoping for positive developments. Many looked to music to provide the answers—or at least a distraction from the real world. People wanted music to reflect the times in which they lived, but they also wanted to use it as a soundtrack to having a good time.

The untimely deaths in 1970 of two of the previous decade's brightest talents, Jimi Hendrix and Janis Joplin, shocked fans and peers alike. Both musicians had given much of themselves for their art and creativity, but the rock 'n' roll lifestyle to which they had grown accustomed

ultimately claimed them, as it did The Doors'
Jim Morrison a year later. Others stared into the
abyss, but did not fall, while some, like the
singer-songwriter Neil Young, felt moved to
comment on the withering effect of drugs on life
and talent in song. The Canadian-born singer's
1971 lament "The Needle and the Damage Done"
was a savage indictment of the destructive
power of drugs.

Passions and ideals

Thankfully, the early 1970s were about more
than dying rock stars. Young's colleagues, David
Crosby, Graham Nash, and Stephen Stills,
carried the banner for well-crafted yet simple
folk-rock songs, blending wonderful harmonies
with pointed lyrics and melodies. While the
sounds that Crosby, Stills, Nash & Young made
were well suited to the hippie ideals of the
1960s—"if you can't be with the one you love,
love the one you're with"—the environment was
such that gentle songs supremely sung could still
make an impression on fans and record sales.

This was the heyday for singer-songwriters on
both sides of the Atlantic. Bob Dylan was at the
height of his creative powers; his 1974 album
Blood on the Tracks was a desperate cry from
the heart over his separation from his wife Sara.
The follow-up, *Desire*, showed he had lost none

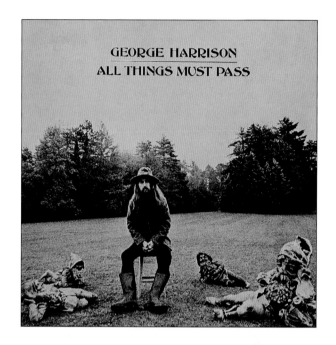

The breakup of The Beatles in the
early 1970s gave George Harrison
the room to grow musically. His
first solo effort after the breakup,
the 1971 triple-disc album *All
Things Must Pass*, showed that
he was much more than just a
background Beatle.

of his wilfulness to speak out against injustice, most notably in the song "Hurricane," which championed a boxer wrongly jailed for murder. The album also brought wider attention to country singer Emmylou Harris, who was a guest vocalist on a number of tracks.

The 1970 album *Bridge Over Troubled Water* was Simon and Garfunkel's crowning achievement, but it also marked the end of the duo's creative partnership.

The tradition of the musician commenting on the surrounding world continued with artists such as Bruce Springsteen, whose observations about blue-collar towns, love, and adventure on the highway of life inspired a number of artists in his wake, including Bob Seger and his Silver Bullet Band. Others, such as Billy Joel, took the singer-songwriter concept a step further and produced commendable, intelligent music that managed to combine goodtime pop with thoughtful lyricism.

Folk and country sounds

James Taylor, a former psychiatric patient turned poet, wrote some of the most affecting folk-rock songs ever recorded around this time, including the classic "Fire and Rain," while John Denver also came to the attention of the record-buying public. Following on from his success as a songwriter—he had penned Peter, Paul and Mary's hit, "Leaving on a Jet Plane"—Denver forged a successful career as a pop-country singer; his gentle, inoffensive balladeering garnered him a huge fanbase and millions of records sold.

A "true" exponent of country music, Willie Nelson, finally saw his own ship come in with two hit albums, a satisfying acknowledgment that those performing the genre could remain true to its roots and still reach a wider audience.

In the UK, singer-songwriter Cat Stevens made his recording comeback with two albums inside a year (*Tea for the Tillerman* and *Teaser and the Firecat*) and took the US by storm with his own brand of pop folk on songs such as "Father and Son" and "Moonshadow."

The British connection

Meanwhile, heavy rock came into its own, thanks largely to British bands such as Led Zeppelin, Deep Purple, and the Ozzy Osborne-fronted Black Sabbath. Led Zeppelin accounted for 64 million album sales in the 1970s—one in 12 of every Top-100-selling album sold—with each of the seven albums the band released in the period topping the charts in the UK and getting a Top Two placing in the US. Black Sabbath and Deep Purple, meanwhile, were content to grind out simple but effective rock classics, such as "Paranoid" and "Smoke on the Water"—songs to bludgeon the senses and storm the charts.

There was more, though, to the UK's rock invasion of the US than a bunch of galvanizing riffs and heavy bass lines. Pink Floyd captured fans with their deeply constructed compositions, heaping electronic sounds onto guitars and keyboards. Jethro Tull's *Aqualung* was another convention-defying album, succeeding in America thanks to its very "British" sound.

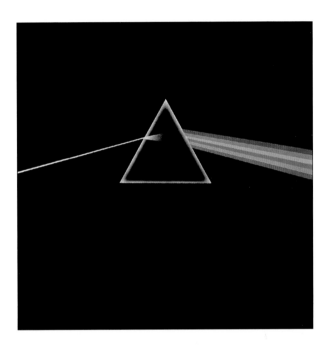

Pink Floyd's 1973 masterpiece *Dark Side of the Moon* remained on the charts for several years after its release in March 1973 and continues to sell well today. The album's innovative, multilayered production techniques proved extremely influential.

Excess all areas

The 1970s was a successful period for UK acts and artists across all genres in the US. Elton John scored three big-hitting releases, starting with his classic album *Don't Shoot Me I'm Only the Piano Player*, while The Rolling Stones continued to have huge success with albums such as *Sticky Fingers*, *Goat's Head Soup*, and the 1978 smash, *Some Girls*. Rod Stewart, who had made a name for himself with his band The Faces and a slew of acclaimed solo albums, extended his career in America with hits such as "Do Ya Think I'm Sexy," which latched onto the craze for all things disco.

Some of the flamboyance of UK glam rock found its way into the big-seller lists through bands such as Queen, whose masterful trio of albums, *A Night at the Opera*, *A Day at the Races*, and *News of the World*, spawned classics such as "Bohemian Rhapsody," "We Are the Champions," and "We Will Rock You."

It was also the time of the "supergroup," nowadays a byword for self-indulgence, but then an indication of musicians wanting to push the creative envelope. Out of Free and Mott the Hoople came Bad Company, while from Spooky Tooth and—once again—Mott the Hoople, came Anglo-American band Foreigner, one of the most successful rock bands of the 1970s and early 1980s. For some, particularly in the UK, Foreigner's polished, glossily produced rock 'n' roll held little attraction, but many others lapped it up, as they did with other "corporate rock" acts such as Chicago's Styx and Boston—whose first radio-friendly album remains to this day a classic AOR (album-oriented rock) record.

Hard rockers

The 1970s also witnessed the rise of a new breed of rock act. Influenced by the hard sounds of established bands like The Rolling Stones, groups such as New Hampshire's Aerosmith challenged the supremacy of UK bands in the field of rock in America. While initially too derivative for some—frontmen Steve Tyler and Joe Perry having more than a passing resemblance to Mick Jagger and Keith Richards—Aerosmith soon developed a hard rock/blues sound of their own. After an initial period as a niche rock outfit, they were to achieve significant mainstream success with a series of single smashes. Lynyrd Skynyrd, meanwhile, took the blues of the Deep South, added some boogie of their own, and made classics such as "Sweet Home Alabama" and "Freebird" before their star crashed to earth.

Scottish-Aussie rockers AC/DC finally saw the pieces of their own career jigsaw fall into place when they broke the US with *Highway To Hell* and, later, their magnificent opus, *Dirty Deeds Done Dirt Cheap*, which had been released in the UK some five years earlier. Sadly, Bon Scott, the band's original frontman, was to die in February 1980, never to savor the success the band had sought for so long.

The Californian band Van Halen were another new act to hit the ground running. Their debut eponymous album, released at the beginning of 1978, knocked the wind out of people who had thought there was little more to be done in rock music. Crucially, much of Van Halen's subsequent success was the result of their positioning themselves as a credible rock band with significant crossover potential, a stand confirmed by hits such as their electrically charged version of The Kinks' "You Really Got Me" and later "Dance the Night Away." The album also sounded uncannily as if it had been recorded live, thanks to the efforts of producer Ted Templeman.

Smoother sounds

Other acts whose high production values were matched by their ability to turn out albums full of searingly good songs included the Anglo-US band Fleetwood Mac, rejuvenated by the arrival in 1975 of singer-songwriter Stevie Nicks and her partner—in music and, at that time, in life—

The Rolling Stones' 1971 album *Sticky Fingers*, with its Andy Warhol-designed sleeve featuring a real jeans zipper, summed up the band's provocative approach to rock—an attitude that was to be adopted by US bands such as Aerosmith.

guitarist and composer Lindsey Buckingham. The new-look band's first offering, 1975's *Fleetwood Mac*, captured imaginations on both sides of the Atlantic, especially a stunning song written and sung by Nicks called "Rhiannon." This record set the scene for the success of their next album, *Rumours*, two years later. A Number One album in the US and the UK, *Rumours* went on to become the third-biggest-selling long-playing record of the decade.

Smooth rock was also a forte of The Eagles. At the outset, the band had a distinctly country vibe, but as the albums came and went they developed a sharper sound, nowhere more in evidence than on their career highlight, *Hotel California*. A biting satire on the American way of life, *Hotel California* also spawned some of the best-loved AOR hits of the time, notably the title track, plus songs such as "New Kid in Town" and "Life in the Fast Lane."

Funk and soul

Proponents of AOR and its ilk did not have everything their own way. Funk and soul made a huge impact during this time, with artists such as Stevie Wonder and Marvin Gaye taking their music into another dimension. Wonder produced songs such as "Superstition," "You Are the Sunshine of My Life," and "Sir Duke,"

while Gaye took the first of many steps into a more politicized style, with albums such as *What's Goin' On* and the sexually charged *Let's Get It On*. Earth, Wind & Fire, meanwhile, scored a number of hits in the 1970s with vibrant, goodtime funk and upbeat soul interpretations.

Evolving genres

The concept album, a child of the 1960s, was reinvented in the 1970s thanks to Jim Steinman and his opus *Bat Out of Hell*, an epic album that enabled the singer Meat Loaf to become something more than a bit player in *The Rocky Horror Picture Show*.

While artists labored to produce their masterworks, the 1970s also saw the first highly successful exploitation of movie soundtracks, compilations featuring music from hit films of the day. *Saturday Night Fever* was one of the most successful, helping define the sound of disco and securing an astounding seven US Number Ones. Two other soundtracks from the decade made a big impression on the charts: Barbra Streisand and Kris Kristofferson's contribution to the remake of *A Star Is Born*, which gave the world "Evergreen"; and the soundtrack to the film of the hit stage show *Grease*, which confirmed John Travolta's status as a pin-up.

As the 1970s drew to a close, America woke up to new wave, with New York bands like The Cars and Blondie proving that sharp, poppy, alternative rock was not the exclusive preserve of bands from London or Manchester.

Another phenomenon that was to stretch into the 1980s and 1990s took shape as the decade neared its end. Michael Jackson released his eight-million-selling commercial behemoth *Off the Wall*, setting the standard for dance-pop music for years to come and turning the 21-year-old singer into a global superstar.

A golden decade

It can be argued that the 1970s witnessed a greater breadth and variety of music than any period before or since. Certainly the evolution of music during this time—the speed with which it changed throughout those ten years—resulted in a great swathe of different sounds.

There was a readiness on the part of the average music fan to listen to different sorts of music. This was, after all, a time before radio formatting took hold of the airwaves and established creative ghettos. This was an era when an album could work its way up the charts and build upon a groundswell of support.

The 1970s were indeed a golden age for popular music in all its many forms.

Michael Jackson's seminal album *Off the Wall* was released in August 1979, providing a taste of what was to come over the next decade. At the time it was the fastest-selling album ever.

100 L.A. Woman

| • **Album sales:** 2,250,000 | • **Release date:** May 1971 |

The sheer creative quality of *L.A. Woman* is all the more remarkable given the point in The Doors' career at which it was recorded and released. Tensions between band members had been rising and frontman Jim Morrison's behavior had become increasingly erratic, thanks to by now well-documented bouts of drinking and drug-taking, as well as police arrests. Many could have been forgiven for thinking that The Doors were a spent force by the time that *L.A. Woman* appeared.

This makes the undoubted power of the album even more notable. Songs such as "Love Her Madly," the epic "Riders on the Storm," the title track—with its saloon-bar honky-tonk piano—

and "L'America" are simply classic Doors tracks.

Morrison's earthy and mature vocal performance is probably as good as any he gave during The Doors' lifetime, and the exemplary nature of the singer's contribution was given added poignancy when he died in Paris a month after the album's release, aged 27.

Upon its release, the album reached Number Nine in the US, spending 34 weeks on the charts. It only managed Number 24 in the UK, but has since become regarded as one of the band's best works. In 1987, it was certified double-platinum and was chosen by a panel of rock critics for *Rolling Stone* magazine as the 92nd greatest rock album of all time.

Number One singles:
None

Grammy Awards: None

Label: US & UK: Elektra

Recorded in: Los Angeles, USA

Personnel:
Jim Morrison
Robby Krieger
Ray Manzarek
John Densmore
Jerry Scheff
Marc Benno

Producers:
Bruce Botnick
The Doors

1. The Changeling (4:20)
2. Love Her Madly (3:18)
3. Been Down So Long (4:40)
4. Cars Hiss By My Window (4:10)
5. L.A. Woman (7:49)
6. L'America (4:35)
7. Hyacinth House (3:10)
8. Crawling King Snake (4:57)
9. The WASP (Texas Radio and the Big Beat) (4:12)
10. Riders on the Storm (7:14)

Total album length: 48 minutes

DOORS

L.A.WOMAN

99 Desire

| • **Album sales:** 2,250,000 | • **Release date:** January 1976 |

The sense of injustice that had fired up the young Bob Dylan in the 1960s was reborn on 1976's *Desire*, where he rediscovers his hunger to champion the underdog.

Released at the end of a purple period for the artist that had produced *Planet Waves* and his divorce album *Blood on the Tracks*, *Desire* finds Dylan the acute topical observer on life, albeit in a musically haphazard way.

The eight-and-a-half-minute opening track "Hurricane" illustrated that his political awareness was still fully intact, rallying against what he saw as the unjust life sentence handed down to former middleweight boxer Rubin "Hurricane"

Carter for triple murder. It was one of seven tracks on the album with lyrics cowritten by playwright Jacques Levy, whom Dylan had met seven years earlier through Roger McGuinn and whose presence here gives the songs a narrative feel. Among the two individually penned tracks is "Sara," Dylan's last plea to his wife, whom he had savagely torn into on a number of tracks on his 1975 album *Blood on the Tracks*.

Including Eric Clapton on guitar and Emmylou Harris on backing vocals, the album became only Dylan's second to top the chart on both sides of the Atlantic, spending a career-best five weeks at Number One in the US from February 1976.

Number One singles:
None

Grammy Awards: None

Label: US: Columbia;
UK: CBS

Recorded in: New York, USA

Personnel:
Bob Dylan
Rob Stoner
Scarlett Rivera
Dom Cortese
Howie Wyeth
Emmylou Harris
Steven Soles

Producer:
Don DeVito

1. Hurricane (8:32)
2. Isis (6:58)
3. Mozambique (3:01)
4. One More Cup of Coffee (Valley Below) (3:47)
5. Oh, Sister (4:03)
6. Joey (11:05)
7. Romance in Durango (5:44)
8. Black Diamond Bay (7:30)
9. Sara (5:31)

Total album length: 56 minutes

98 After the Gold Rush

• Album sales: 2,350,000 | **• Release date:** September 1970

Mixing folk rock with the harder sound that comes from Neil Young's occasional collaborations with backing band Crazy Horse, the Canadian singer-songwriter's third solo album was released just six months after *Déjà Vu*, his first with Crosby, Stills & Nash.

With the exception of a cover of country singer Don Gibson's 1957 hit "Oh, Lonesome Me," all of the songs are by Young, with most, including the title track, inspired by an unproduced, apocalypse-themed screenplay by Dean Stockwell and Herb Bermann.

Young has never been much of a name for hits—the album's highest-charting single was "Only Love Can Break Your Heart," which reached Number 33 in the *Billboard* charts—but *After the Gold Rush* stands out as an album of consistently strong country folk and rock songs.

The title track, recorded with just Young's vocal, piano, and session musician Bill Peterson's mournful flugelhorn, has become one of the singer's best-known and most-covered songs, while "Southern Man," with its excoriating lyrics about the South's history of slavery, prompted Lynyrd Skynyrd to respond with their 1974 song "Sweet Home Alabama."

Number One singles:
None

Grammy Awards: None

Label: Reprise

Recorded in: Topanga and Los Angeles, California, USA

Producer:
Neil Young

David Briggs
Kendall Pacios

Personnel:
Neil Young
Danny Whitten
Nils Lofgren
Jack Nitzsche
Billy Talbot
Greg Reeves
Ralph Molina
Stephen Stills
Bill Peterson

1. Tell Me Why (2:54)
2. After the Gold Rush (3:45)
3. Only Love Can Break Your Heart (3:05)
4. Southern Man (5:31)
5. Till the Morning Comes (1:17)
6. Oh, Lonesome Me (3:47)
7. Don't Let It Bring You Down (2:56)
8. Birds (2:34)
9. When You Dance I Can Really Love (4:05)
10. I Believe in You (3:23)
11. Cripple Creek Ferry (1:34)

Total album length: 35 minutes

AFTER THE GOLD RUSH · NEIL YOUNG

Sleeve artwork by Gary Burden; cover photograph by Joel Bernstein

97 Blood on the Tracks

| • **Album sales:** 2,500,000 | • **Release date:** January 1975 |

An intensely touching album from an artist at the height of his powers, *Blood on the Tracks* is essentially about a marriage breakdown; in this case, that of Dylan's own to his wife, Sara. Songs such as "You're Gonna Make Me Lonesome When You Go," "You're a Big Girl Now," and "If You See Her, Say Hello" speak for themselves in terms of regret and lamenting love lost, while "Buckets of Rain" is a bittersweet love song. Throughout the album, the perfect cadence of Dylan's poetry barely disguises his rage—anger that really comes to the fore in songs such as "Idiot Wind." Dylan also manages to weave examples of his trademark epic folk stories into his songs, as evidenced on the relatively upbeat "Lily, Rosemary and the Jack of Hearts."

The album is also notable for having been almost completed over a series of recording sessions that were subsequently scrapped by Dylan in favor of re-recording with a different group of musicians.

Blood on the Tracks topped the US charts and managed a Number Four placing in the UK. In "Tangled Up in Blue" it also gave Dylan his biggest US single hit since "Knockin' on Heaven's Door" two years earlier.

Number One singles:
None

Grammy Awards: None

Label: US: Columbia;
UK: CBS

Recorded in: New York &
Minneapolis, USA

Producer:
Bob Dylan

Personnel:
Bob Dylan
Tony Brown
Buddy Cage
Paul Griffin
Ken Odeguard
Bill Berg
Barry Kornfeld
Greg Inhofer
Billy Peterson
Eric Weissberg

1. Tangled Up in Blue (5:42)
2. Simple Twist of Fate (4:19)
3. You're a Big Girl Now (4:36)
4. Idiot Wind (7:49)
5. You're Gonna Make Me Lonesome When You Go (2:55)
6. Meet Me in the Morning (4:22)
7. Lily, Rosemary and the Jack of Hearts (8:53)
8. If You See Her, Say Hello (4:49)
9. Shelter From the Storm (5:02)
10. Buckets of Rain (3:22)

Total album length: 52 minutes

BOB
DYLAN
BLOOD
ON
THE
TRACKS

96 Dire Straits

| • **Album sales:** 2,650,000 | • **Release date:** October 1978 |

The British rock band's debut, *Dire Straits* made the Top Five in both the UK and the *Billboard* Hot 100, reached Number One in France and Australia, and, in all, spent more than two years on the UK albums chart.

Formed in 1977, Dire Straits comprised songwriter, lead guitarist, and lead vocalist Mark Knopfler, his younger brother David on rhythm guitar, John Illsley on bass, and Pick Withers on drums.

With his wry, conversational lyrics and commonplace voice, Mark Knopfler has been compared to Bob Dylan, but Dire Straits differed in Knopfler's virtuoso guitar playing and their larger, rootsier sound.

The band sent their first five-song demo to Charlie Gillett at BBC Radio London, seeking only his advice, but, liking what he heard, the DJ began playing their track "Sultans of Swing" on his show.

Knopfler had been inspired to write the song on witnessing a jazz band announce themselves as "the sultans of swing," despite their unremarkable appearance and the fact that they were performing in a near-empty pub in Deptford, southeast London. Such was the response from listeners that within two months Dire Straits had signed a major recording contract and could give up their day jobs.

Over the years, the lineup of Dire Straits would change, with only Mark Knopfler and John Illsley lasting throughout.

Number One singles:
None

Grammy Awards:
None

Label: US: Warner Bros.
UK: Vertigo

Recorded in: London, UK

Personnel:
Mark Knopfler
David Knopfler
John Illsley
Pick Withers

Producer:
Muff Winwood

1. **Down to the Waterline** (3:55)
2. **Water of Love** (5:23)
3. **Setting Me Up** (3:18)
4. **Six Blade Knife** (4:10)
5. **Southbound Again** (2:58)
6. **Sultans of Swing** (5:47)
7. **In the Gallery** (6:16)
8. **Wild West End** (4:42)
9. **Lions** (5:05)

Total album length: 41 minutes

Dire Straits

DIRE STRAITS

95 The War of the Worlds

| • **Album sales:** 2,750,000 | • **Release date:** September 1978 |

Based on H.G. Wells's 1898 novel about a Martian invasion, *Jeff Wayne's Musical Version of The War of the Worlds* is a concept album mixing progressive rock and a string orchestra.

With musical leitmotifs and songs—the lyrics were mainly written by English lyricist Gary Osborne—the album also features many moments of spoken word supplied by the singers and also by actor Richard Burton as the narrator.

Vocals were handled by The Moody Blues's Justin Hayward, Thin Lizzy's Phil Lynott, David Essex, and Julie Covington.

The single "Forever Autumn" reached Number Five in the UK, but only 47 in the US. Nevertheless, it was the album that was the draw, spending 290 weeks on the UK album charts and reaching Number One in 11 countries.

Although *The War of the Worlds* is considered Wayne's debut album, the American had been active for a decade in London as a record producer and composer of stage musicals, TV theme songs, and advertising jingles.

In subsequent years, Wayne has toured the album with different casts, while in 2012 he even revised the music itself for *War of the Worlds— The New Generation*.

Number One singles:
None

Grammy Awards: None

Label: US & UK:
Columbia/CBS Records

Recorded in: London, UK

Producer:
Jeff Wayne

Personnel:
Jeff Wayne
Chris Spedding
Herbie Flowers
Ken Freeman
Barry Morgan
Richard Burton
Justin Hayward
David Essex
Chris Thompson
Phil Lynott
Julie Covington
Jerry Wayne

1. The Eve of the War (9:07)
2. Horsell Common and the Heat Ray (11:35)
3. The Artilleryman and the Fighting Machine (10:37)
4. Forever Autumn (7:55)
5. Thunder Child (6:03)
6. The Red Weed (5:51)
7. The Spirit of Man (11:45)
8. The Red Weed (6:19)
9. Brave New World (12:36)
10. Dead London (8:36)
11. Epilogue (Part 1) (2:42)
12. Epilogue (Part 2) (2:01)

Total album length: 95 minutes

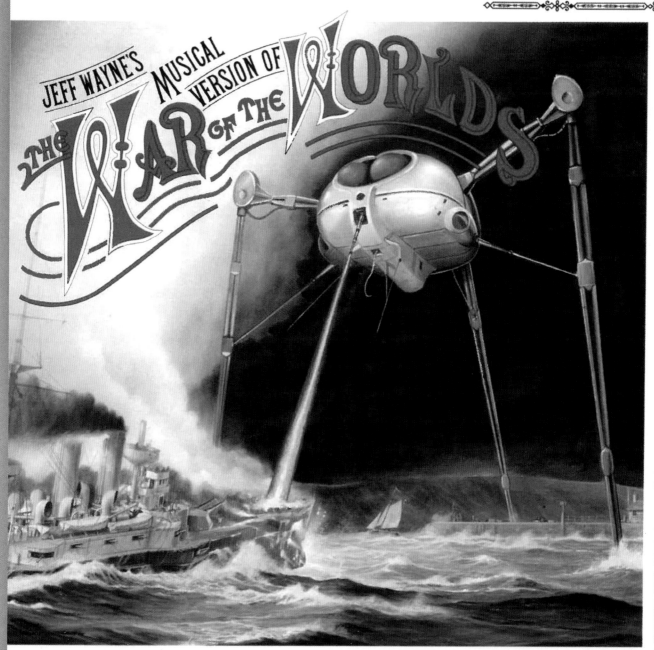

94 A Song For You

| • **Album sales:** 3,050,000 | • **Release date:** September 1972 |

The Carpenters hit such creative form with *A Song For You* that it ended up being mined for more singles than any other of the brother-sister duo's studio recordings.

By the time of its release in June 1972, the combination of Richard and Karen's wholesome image and their unthreatening yet popular melodies had turned them into major stars, but here the inconsistencies of their earlier albums are replaced by one quality cut after another. One vital contributor to the formula is lyricist John Bettis, who cowrote with Richard two of the album's most famous tracks, the US Top 10 hit "Goodbye to Love" and "Top of the World,"

which Richard deemed worthy only as an album cut, although it went on to head the Hot 100 nearly a year and a half after the album's release.

Richard's knack of picking the right material for him and Karen to cover is evident on "Hurting Each Other," originally recorded by Ruby & The Romantics, becoming a Number Two US hit, and a then new Carole King song, "It's Going to Take Some Time," reaching the Top 20.

"I Won't Last a Day Without You," penned by regular Carpenters' contributors Paul Williams and Roger Nichols, completes the album's quota of hits. The album peaked at Number Four in the US in July 1972, and at Number 13 in the UK.

Number One singles:
None

Grammy Awards: None

Label: US & UK: A&M

Recorded in: N/A

Producer:
Jack Daugherty

Personnel:
Karen Carpenter
Richard Carpenter
Joe Osborn
Hal Blaine
Bob Messenger
Tim Weisberg
Louie Shelton
Tony Peluso
Red Rhodes
Earle Dumler
Norm Herzberg

1. A Song For You (4:42)
2. Top of the World (2:59)
3. Hurting Each Other (2:48)
4. It's Going to Take Some Time (2:56)
5. Goodbye to Love (3:58)
6. Intermission (0:26)
7. Bless the Beasts and Children (3:09)
8. Flat Baroque (1:48)
9. Piano Picker (2:01)
10. I Won't Last a Day Without You (3:52)
11. Crystal Lullaby (3:55)
12. Road Ode (3:44)
13. A Song For You (Reprise) (0:55)

Total album length: 37 minutes

93 An Evening With John Denver

| • **Album sales:** 3,050,000 | • **Release date:** March 1975 |

Following 1974's *Back Home Again* came the live double offering *An Evening With John Denver*, recorded at the California Universal Amphitheatre with full orchestral backing. This is Denver at his wholesome best, with feelgood songs such as "Farewell Andromeda (Welcome to My Morning)," The Beatles' cover of "Mother Nature's Son," and a run-through of many of his best-known songs, including "Rocky Mountain High"—which celebrates Aspen, Colorado—and "Take Me Home, Country Roads."

In combining a style of soft pop and folk with tinges of country (certainly in subject matter), Denver fell uncomfortably between several stools. Country music was never entirely happy to claim him as one of its own, best illustrated when he won the Country Music Association Entertainer of the Year Award in 1975 and Charlie Rich, in announcing the award, produced a cigarette lighter and incinerated the winners' list that he was holding. *An Evening With John Denver* reached Number Three in the US and a more modest Number 31 position in the UK.

Number One singles:
None

Grammy Awards: None

Label: US & UK: RCA Victor

Recorded in: California, USA

Personnel:
John Denver
Steve Weisberg
Dick Kniss
John Sommers
Hal Blaine
Lee Holdridge
Richard Kniss
Herb Lovelle

Producer:
Milton Okun

1. Music is You (1:01)
2. Farewell Andromeda (Welcome to My Morning) (5:46)
3. Mother Nature's Son (2:26)
4. Summer (3:02)
5. Today (6:23)
6. Toledo (2:30)
7. Matthew (3:51)
8. Rocky Mountain Suite (Cold Nights in Canada) (3:15)
9. Sweet Surrender (5:03)
10. Grandma's Feather Bed (2:35)
11. Annie's Song (3:35)
12. Eagle and the Hawk (2:20)
13. My Sweet Lady (4:55)
14. Annie's Other Song (3:05)
15. Boy From the Country (5:01)
16. Rhymes and Reasons (3:19)
17. Forest Lawn (3:04)
18. Pickin' the Sun Down (2:17)
19. Thank God I'm a Country Boy (3:40)
20. Take Me Home, Country Roads (3:18)
21. Poems, Prayers and Promises (4:41)
22. Rocky Mountain High (5:04)
23. This Old Guitar (5:00)

Total album length:
1 hour 25 minutes

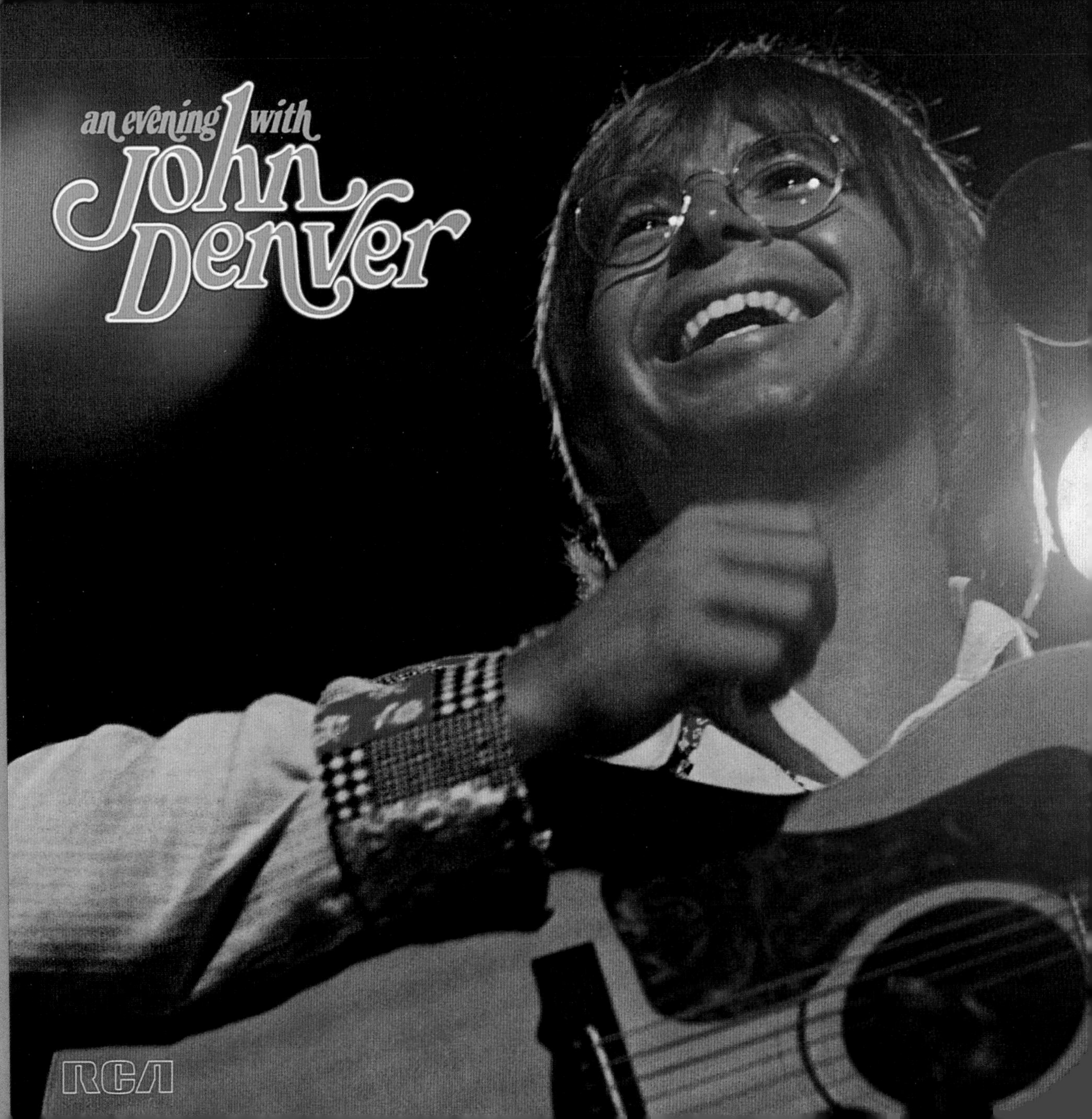
an evening with
John Denver
RCA

92 JT

• **Album sales:** 3,050,000 | • **Release date:** July 1977 |

The singer's first album for his new record company, *JT* is an assertion, indeed a defense almost, of the "new" James Taylor, an artist who is full of the joys of spring and exuding an almost unfamiliar confidence.

Having established himself as one of the most respected and prominent US singer-songwriters, Taylor appears to want, if not to exactly reinvent himself with his new employers, then at least to illustrate another side to his talents. The upbeat numbers, such as "Honey Don't Leave L.A." and "Your Smiling Face" reinforce this, while the slick production from long-time producer Peter Asher, and the retention of long-time backing musicians Danny Kortchmar (who penned "Honey Don't Leave L.A."), Russ Kunkel, and Leland Sklar maintain the musical continuity.

There are still trademark Taylor tunes here, with ballads in "Secret o' Life" and "If I Keep My Heart Out of Sight." The album's opener, and a Number 20 hit in the US, "Your Smiling Face" is a declaration of love for Taylor's wife, singer Carly Simon, as is the record's second cut, "There We Are." Fans embraced the record, sending it to the Number Four position on the US album chart. The song "Handy Man" won Taylor a Grammy in the Best Pop Vocal Performance category.

Number One singles:
None

Grammy Awards:
Best Pop Vocal
Performance

Label: US: Columbia;
UK: CBS

Recorded in:
Los Angeles, USA

Personnel:
James Taylor
Leland Sklar
Dr Clarence McDonald
Danny Kortchmar
Russell Kunkel
Carly Simon
Linda Ronstadt
David Sanborn

Producer:
Peter Asher

1. Your Smiling Face (2:47)
2. There We Are (3:00)
3. Honey Don't Leave L.A. (3:06)
4. Another Grey Morning (2:44)
5. Bartender's Blues (4:12)
6. Secret o'Life (3:35)
7. Handy Man (3:18)
8. I Was Only Telling a Lie (3:24)
9. Looking For Love on Broadway (2:21)
10. Terra Nova (4:32)
11. Traffic Jam (1:58)
12. If I Keep My Heart Out of Sight (2:58)

Total album length: 38 minutes

JT

Sleeve artwork by Kosh, Jim Shea, and David Alexander

91 Simple Dreams

| • **Album sales:** 3,050,000 | • **Release date:** November 1977 |

Simple Dreams was the latest chapter in a highly effective formula of hit remakes and new material that had lifted Linda Ronstadt to superstar status by the mid-1970s.

Ronstadt and her manager-producer Peter Asher had hit upon the magic ingredients with such stunning effect on her breakthrough 1974 album *Heart Like A Wheel* that they stuck to the pattern for her subsequent albums. Opener "It's So Easy" became a US Top Five smash and her third Buddy Holly remake to reach the Hot 100 in just over two years, while her reinterpretation of Roy Orbison's "Blue Bayou" landed her a first million-selling single. Elsewhere, she covered The Rolling Stones on "Tumbling Dice" and exposed then fledgling Warren Zevon's work to its widest audience yet with versions of his "Poor, Poor Pitiful Me" and the Mexican-styled "Carmelita." There is also room for a couple of self-penned tunes, including "I Never Will Marry," on which she duets with Dolly Parton.

Simple Dreams became Ronstadt's second US chart-topping album, replacing Fleetwood Mac's *Rumours* at Number One in December 1977 and staying there for a career-peaking five weeks; it managed Number 15 in the UK.

Number One singles:
None

Grammy Awards:
Album Package

Label: US & UK: Asylum

Recorded in: Los Angeles, USA

Personnel:
Linda Ronstadt
Mike Auldridge
Dolly Parton
Karla Bonoff
Don Henley
Don Grolnick
Andrew Gold
Peter Asher
David Campbell
Charles Veal
Dan Dugmore
Kenny Edwards
Richard Feves
Steve Forman
Jim Gilstrap
Larry Hagler
Pat Henderson
Various other personnel

Producer:
Peter Asher

1. It's So Easy (2:27)
2. Carmelita (3:07)
3. Simple Man, Simple Dream (3:12)
4. Sorrow Lives Here (2:57)
5. I Never Will Marry (3:12)
6. Blue Bayou (3:57)
7. Poor, Poor Pitiful Me (3:42)
8. Maybe I'm Right (3:05)
9. Tumbling Dice (3:05)
10. Old Paint (3:05)

Total album length: 31 minutes

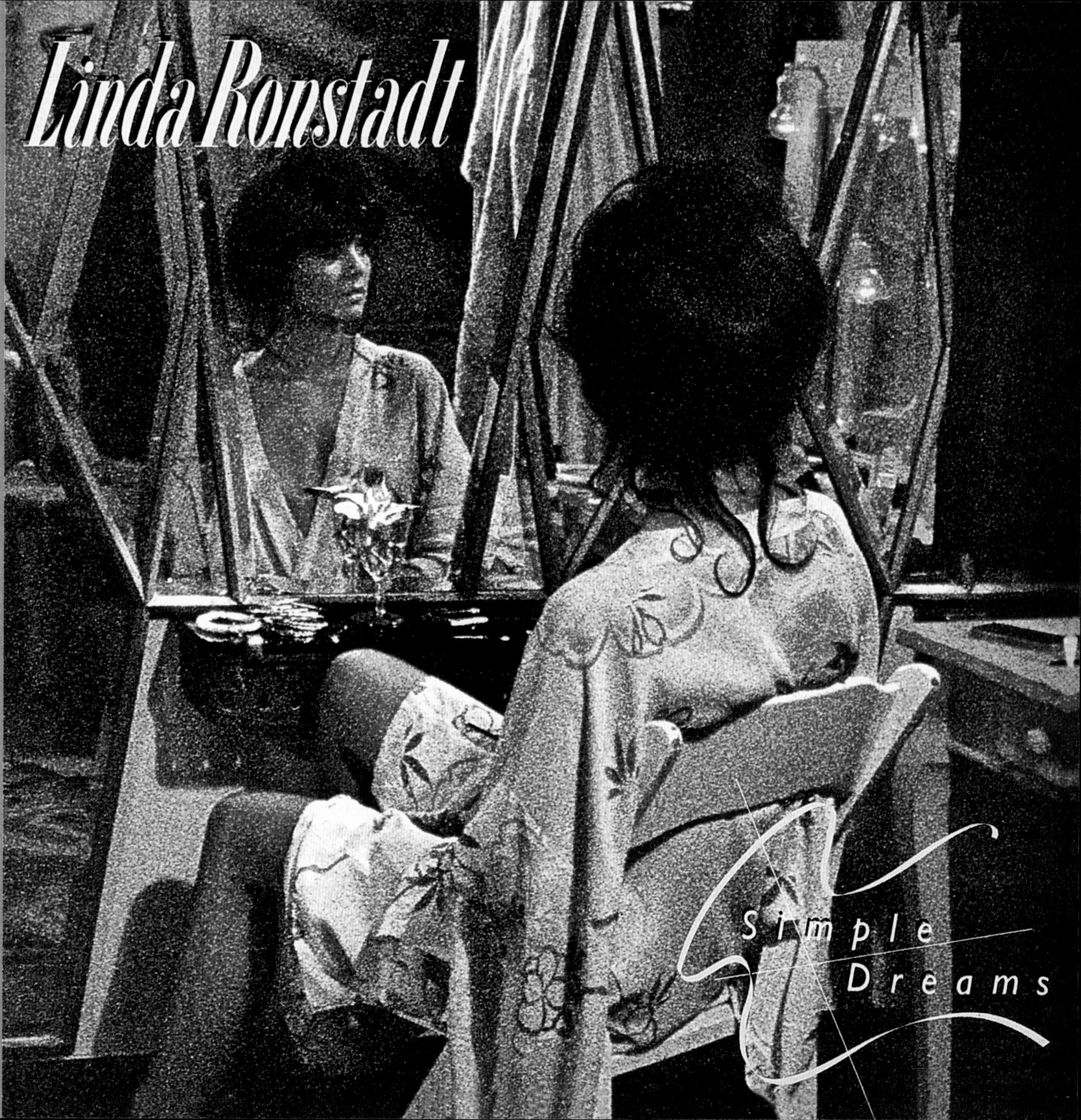
Linda Ronstadt
Simple
Dreams

90 Pieces of Eight

| • **Album sales:** 3,050,000 | • **Release date:** September 1978 |

Coming off a two-year, 400-date tour and the triple-hit single, triple-platinum *The Grand Illusion*, Styx consolidated their success with 1978's *Pieces of Eight*, which reached Number Six on the US album chart. The album boasted two hit singles: the US Number 21 "Blue Collar Man (Long Nights)" and the Number 16-peaking "Renegade." "Blue Collar Man"—inspired by the memories of a then-unemployed Tommy Shaw—featured a Hammond organ sound and twirling guitar riff, which, if it didn't exactly doff its cap to Deep Purple, certainly anticipates the hit singles of Rainbow, the group that Deep Purple's Ritchie Blackmore later founded.

The jaunty, jogging "Renegade" follows a similar path, but the band stretch out more—or perhaps back to an earlier sound—on the complex balladry of "I'm OK," while returning to their progressive roots on "Sing for the Day." *Pieces of Eight* is something of a crossroads: AOR is beckoning on the hit singles, but elsewhere the prog blueprint is still fluttering, no more so than on "I'm OK," which features a pipe organ solo by Dennis DeYoung, recorded at Chicago's Cathedral of St James.

The album sleeve was designed by Storm Thorgerson and Hipgnosis, who also worked on many Pink Floyd and Led Zeppelin album covers and were responsible for some of the decade's most iconic album images.

Number One singles:
None

Grammy Awards: None

Label: US & UK: A&M

Recorded in: Chicago, USA

Personnel:
Dennis DeYoung
Chuck Panozzo
John Panozzo
Tommy Shaw
James "JY" Young

Producers:
Styx

1. Great White Hope (4:22)
2. I'm OK (5:41)
3. Sing for the Day (4:57)
4. The Message (1:08)
5. Lords of the Ring (4:33)
6. Blue Collar Man (Long Nights) (4:05)
7. Queen of Spades (5:38)
8. Renegade (4:13)
9. Pieces of Eight (4:44)
10. Aku-Aku (2:57)

Total album length: 42 minutes

Styx

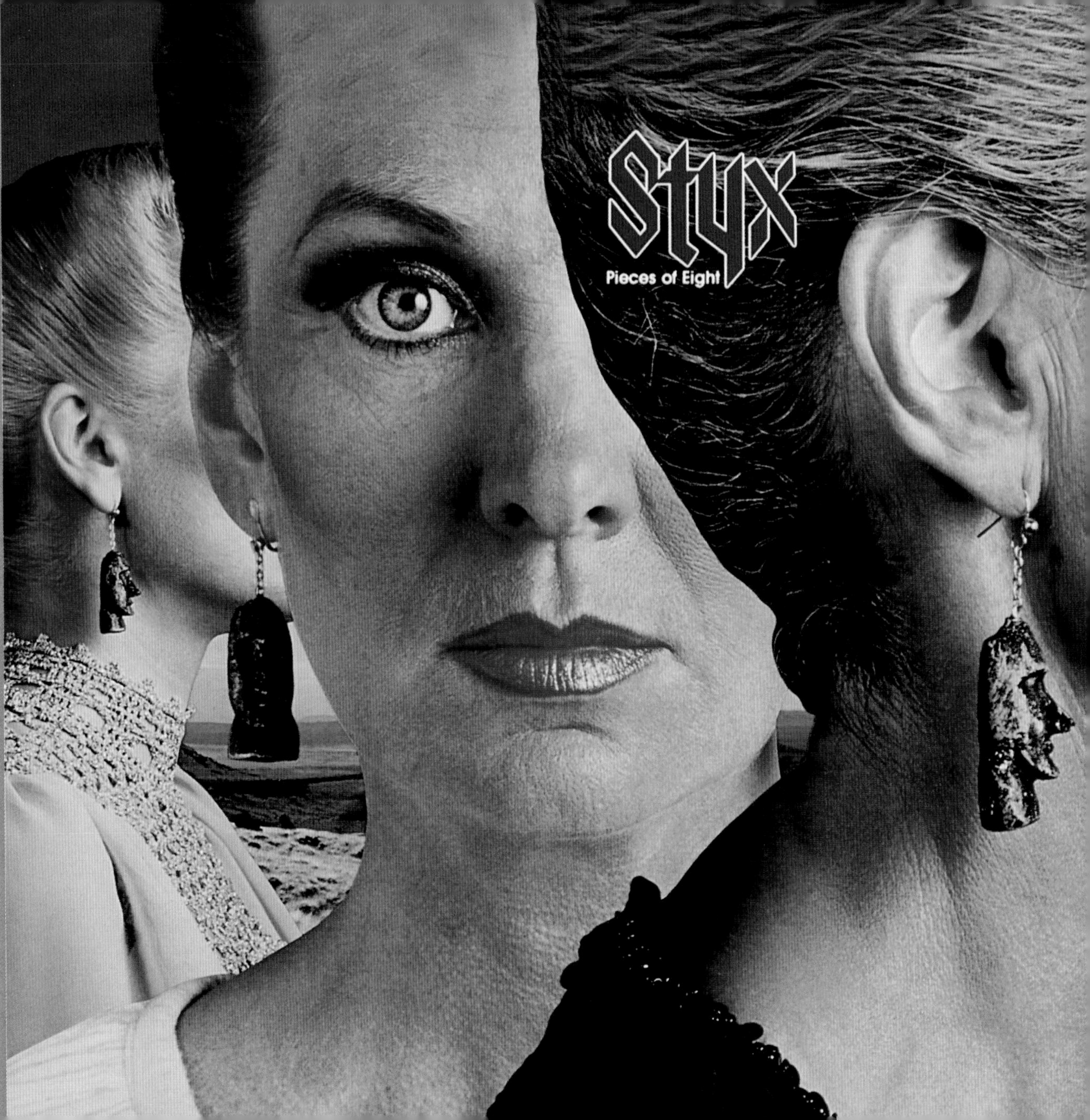

Styx

Pieces of Eight

89 Minute By Minute

| • **Album sales:** 3,050,000 | • **Release date:** December 1978 |

The second Doobie Brothers album to be recorded without founding member Tom Johnston—who had retired from the band due to ill health—*Minute By Minute* is a classy blend of West Coast rock, melodic pop, and white soul, thanks in no small part to Michael McDonald's soaring vocals.

With a funkier outlook and more polished sound than previous Doobie records, tracks such as the title song, "Open Your Eyes," "Dependin' on You," and "You Never Change" are slick in their composition, playing, and production.

"What a Fool Believes" was the first of three Top 40 singles off what would become their eighth gold album of the 1970s. Released in December 1978, *Minute By Minute* became their first Number One album in the US, a position it held for five weeks; in total it spent 87 weeks on the *Billboard* Hot 200 album chart. In the UK, the record did not even chart.

The album won four Grammys, including Record of the Year and Song of the Year for "What a Fool Believes," which also topped the US singles chart and hovered outside the UK singles countdown at Number 31.

Number One singles:
US: "What a Fool Believes"

Recorded in:
Los Angeles, USA

Grammy Awards: Best Pop Vocal Performance by a Duo, Group, or Chorus; Song of the Year: "What a Fool Believes"; Record of the Year: "What a Fool Believes"; Best Arrangement Accompanying Vocals: "What a Fool Believes"

Personnel:
Patrick Simmons
Michael McDonald
Jeffrey Baxter
Tiran Porter
John Hartman
Keith Knudsen

Producer:
Ted Templeman

Label: Reprise

1. Here To Love You (4:03)
2. What a Fool Believes (3:46)
3. Minute By Minute (3:29)
4. Dependin' on You (3:48)
5. Don't Stop to Watch the Wheels (3:29)
6. Open Your Eyes (3:19)
7. Sweet Feelin' (2:44)
8. Steamer Lane Breakdown (3:27)
9. You Never Change (3:29)
10. How Do the Fools Survive? (5:17)

Total album length: 37 minutes

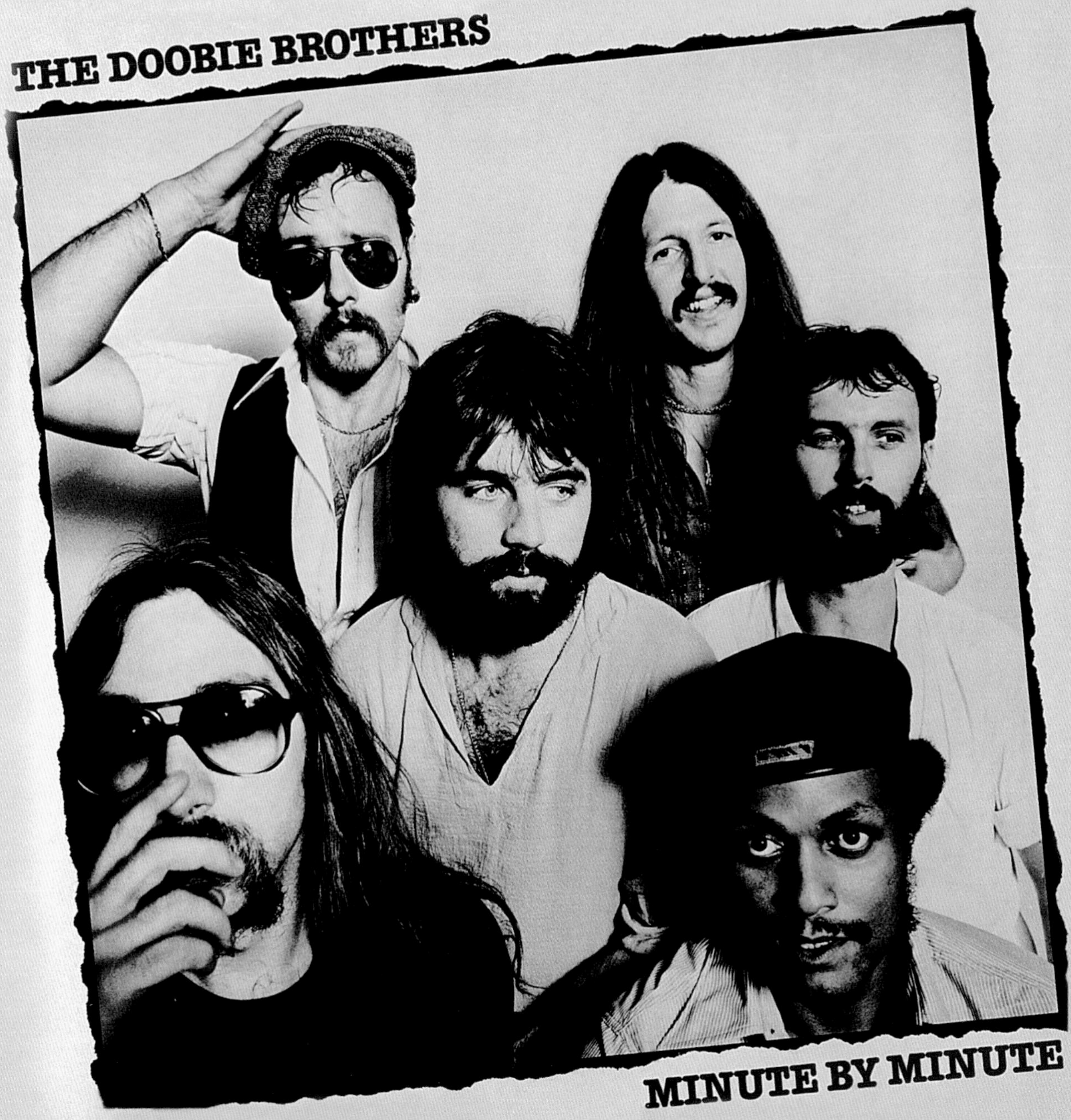

THE DOOBIE BROTHERS
MINUTE BY MINUTE

88 Don't Shoot Me I'm Only the Piano Player

| • **Album sales:** 3,100,000 | • **Release date:** January 1973 |

Elton John's pop sensibilities abundantly came to the fore on *Don't Shoot Me I'm Only the Piano Player*, the success of which sealed the songwriter's status as a genuine superstar.

Recorded in June 1972, the album salutes the artist's love of catchy, goodtime rock 'n' roll, but also offers social commentary via Bernie Taupin's (John's long-time lyricist) lyrics on the likes of "Have Mercy on the Criminal" and "Texan Love Song."

Two of the album's highlights are undoubtedly its pair of singles, "Daniel" and "Crocodile Rock." The former, the set's opening track, is a moving ballad that stands as one of Elton John's greatest, even if its original Vietnam setting is forever lost by a decision to drop the final verse.

By contrast, "Crocodile Rock," which in February 1973 became the singer's first ever Hot 100 Number One, is an unashamed celebration of his boyhood love of rock 'n' roll. Teenage themes are also visited on "Teacher I Need You" and "I'm Gonna Be a Teenage Idol."

Eight months after his first US Number One album with *Honky Château*, *Don't Shoot…* replaced War's *The World is a Ghetto* at the top in March 1973 for a two-week run, while it also topped the UK chart.

Number One singles:
US: "Crocodile Rock"

Grammy Awards: None

Label: US: MCA; UK: DJM

Recorded in: Paris, France

Producer:
Gus Dudgeon

Personnel:
Elton John
Davey Johnstone
Dee Murray
Nigel Olsson
Paul Buckmaster
Jean Louis Chautemps
Alain Hatot
Jacques Bolognesi

1. Daniel (3:53)
2. Teacher I Need You (4:10)
3. Elderberry Wine (3:34)
4. Blues For My Baby and Me (5:39)
5. Midnight Creeper (3:52)
6. Have Mercy on the Criminal (5:58)
7. I'm Gonna Be a Teenage Idol (3:55)
8. Texas Love Song (3:34)
9. Crocodile Rock (3:58)
10. High Flying Bird (4:12)

Total album length: 43 minutes

87 Straight Shooter

| • **Album sales:** 3,100,000 | • **Release date:** April 1975 |

Adhering to the old adage "if it ain't broke, don't fix it," Bad Company's second album continues where their first album left off. Good old-fashioned rock, effectively constructed songs with raucous vocals, guitar breaks in all the right places, bluesy riffs, and solid rhythms, *Straight Shooter* didn't disappoint fans who may have feared the band would seek to travel down new creative avenues.

To record their second album, the band hired former Small Faces bassist Ronnie Lane's mobile recording studio and installed it in the atmospheric surroundings of Clearwell Castle, UK. The results were impressive. The album, like its predecessor, opens strongly, with "Good Lovin' Gone Bad." "Deal With the Preacher" is as ballsy a rock track as any the band had recorded to date. "Feel Like Making Love" rose to Number 10 on the *Billboard* charts, making it the group's biggest hit after "Can't Get Enough," which hit Number Five.

Bad Company later tired of this effective style and moved toward a more melodic, almost AOR, sound, but with *Straight Shooter* they kept it simple and as such it worked for most fans. Although the record didn't match its predecessor in charting terms (their debut album reached Number One), it managed a respectable Number Three spot on the US Hot 100, spending 33 weeks on the charts and achieving the Number Three position in the UK.

Number One singles:
None

Grammy Awards: None

Label: US: Swan Song;
UK: Island

Recorded in: Clearwell
Castle, UK

Personnel:
Paul Rogers
Mick Ralphs
Boz Burrell
Simon Kirke

Producers:
Bad Company

1. **Good Lovin' Gone Bad** (3:37)
2. **Feel Like Makin' Love** (5:16)
3. **Weep No More** (4:02)
4. **Shooting Star** (6:19)
5. **Deal With the Preacher** (5:04)
6. **Wild Fire Woman** (4:35)
7. **Anna** (3:45)
8. **Call on Me** (6:05)

Total album length: 39 minutes

That's the Way of the World

| • **Album sales:** 3,100,000 | • **Release date:** April 1975 |

Earth, Wind & Fire were becoming such hot R&B properties by the mid-1970s that when *Superfly* director Stig Shore was looking to cast a credible group for a new movie they seemed natural choices.

The movie in question, *That's the Way of the World*, in which Shore aimed to expose the payola-ridden music business, spectacularly bombed at the box office, but the accompanying album of the same name set the nine-piece outfit on a path to superstardom that would continue for the rest of the decade.

Recorded over nine months in Nederland, Colorado, the album skilfully blends soul, rock, and Latin rhythms across its eight tracks, all overseen by the band's founder and leader Maurice White. Its lead-off single "Shining Star," showcasing a magnificent falsetto performance from the track's cowriter Philip Bailey, became the group's million-selling singles' breakthrough, the first of eight *Billboard* R&B chart Number Ones and their only Hot 100 chart-topper. It hit the top just a week after *That's the Way of the World* started its own three-week run at Number One in May 1975, making them the first ever R&B act to top both singles and albums countdowns simultaneously.

Number One singles:
US: "Shining Star"

Grammy Awards:
Best R&B Vocal Performance by a Duo, Group, or Chorus

Label: US: Columbia; UK: CBS

Recorded in:
Nederland, Colorado, USA

Personnel:
Maurice White
Philip Bailey
Verdine White
Larry Dunn
Al McKay
Johnny Graham
Andrew Woolfolk
Ralph Johnson
Fred White

Producers:
Maurice White
Charles Stepney

1. **Shining Star** (2:50)
2. **That's the Way of the World** (5:45)
3. **Happy Feelin' (Anatomy of a Groove)** (3:35)
4. **All About Love (First Impressions)** (6:35)
5. **Yearnin', Learnin'** (3:39)
6. **Reasons** (4:59)
7. **Africano** (5:09)
8. **See the Light** (6:18)

Total album length: 39 minutes

85 Gratitude

| • **Album sales:** 3,100,000 | • **Release date:** December 1975 |

Three months before *Frampton Comes Alive!* topped the US chart, Earth, Wind & Fire were setting their own standard for live albums with *Gratitude*. Combining live cuts and new studio recordings, this 1975 double set gives some hint of the fact that, as good as the band were on record, they really excelled in live performances in the 1970s.

Released only a few months after their studio album breakthrough *That's the Way of the World*, *Gratitude* captures Earth, Wind & Fire at the peak of their live powers. "Reasons" combines the astounding voice of Philip Bailey and saxophonist Don Myrick, while there is also room for such fare as a nine-and-a-half-minute instrumental suite, "New World Symphony."

The new studio recordings include another million-seller and *Billboard* R&B Number One, the uplifting dance track "Sing a Song," which became a crossover Top Five hit in early 1976, just as the album moved to Number One in the States for a three-week run.

Given their striking presence as a stage act, *Gratitude* surprisingly stands as the only major-label live album release by the group.

Number One singles:
None

Grammy Awards: None

Label: US: Columbia;
UK: CBS

Recorded in: Los Angeles & various concert locations, USA

Personnel:
Maurice White
Philip Bailey
Ralph Johnson
Fred White
Al McKay
Verdine White
Andrew Woolfolk
John Graham
Larry Dunn

Producers:
Maurice White
Charles Stepney
Joseph Wissert

1. **Introduction By MC Perry Jones** (0:21)
2. **Medley: Africano/Power** (5:56)
3. **Yearnin' Learnin'** (4:16)
4. **Devotion** (5:07)
5. **Sun Goddess** (7:41)
6. **Reasons** (8:23)
7. **Sing a Message to You** (1:19)
8. **Shining Star** (4:16)
9. **New World Symphony** (9:28)
10. **Musical Interlude #1** (0:15)
11. **Sunshine** (4:16)
12. **Sing a Song** (3:23)
13. **Gratitude** (3:27)
14. **Celebrate** (3:06)
15. **Musical Interlude #2** (2:27)
16. **Can't Hide Love** (4:10)

Total album length: 66 minutes

Stereo

Can also be
played on mono
equipment
See note over

CBS

88160

SPECIAL PRICED
2-RECORD SET

EARTH, WIND & FIRE

Gratitude

84 Book of Dreams

| • **Album sales:** 3,100,000 | • **Release date:** May 1977 |

Steve Miller recorded the bulk of *Book of Dreams* at the CBS studios, California, in the same sessions that had yielded the previous year's *Fly Like an Eagle.* Most of the songs on both albums had been written when Miller took a break from touring and retreated to a remote corner of Marin County, California, where he built a home recording studio.

Like its 1976 predecessor, *Book of Dreams* became a multi-platinum seller, peaking at Number Two in the US and providing a Number Eight Hot 100 single in "Jet Airliner." This, Miller's 12th album, also proved popular in the UK, with *Book of Dreams* just failing by one position to match the 1976 breakthrough in reaching Number 12.

While it could be argued that Miller was doing nothing particularly new—the bubbling synthesizer of opener "Threshold" is not especially original, while the "Jet Airliner" single is as standard a track as one could wish to hear—there is an indefinable magic to his music. Miller deserves his success for his role in introducing his San Francisco blues-rock to a wider progressive audience.

Number One singles:
None

Grammy Awards: None

Label: US: Capitol;
UK: Mercury

Recorded in: California,
USA

Personnel:
Steve Miller
Byron Allred
David Denny
Greg Douglass
Lonnie Turner
Gary Mallaber
Led Dudek
Bob Glaub
Bryan Allred
Charles Calmese
Ken Johnson
Norton Buffalo
Curley Cooke

Producers:
Steve Miller
John Palladino

1. Threshold (1:06)
2. Jet Airliner (4:25)
3. Winter Time (3:12)
4. Swingtown (3:56)
5. True Fine Love (2:39)
6. Wish Upon a Star (3:39)
7. Jungle Love (3:07)
8. Electro Lux Imbroglio (0:57)
9. Sacrifice (5:20)
10. The Stake (3:58)
11. My Own Space (3:04)
12. Babes in the Wood (2:32)

Total album length: 38 minutes

THE STEVE MILLER BAND

BOOK OF DREAMS

83 The Grand Illusion

| • **Album sales:** 3,100,000 | • **Release date:** August 1977 |

Styx, with their big, layered harmonies and a kitchen-sink approach to production, for many people epitomize everything that is good—or indeed bad—about AOR. The band's seventh album, *The Grand Illusion,* brought together the various stands of prog, rock, and pomp that would begin a string of four multi-platinum albums for Styx. The album reached Number Six in the US and spent nine months on the *Billboard* chart.

The album includes the Chicago-based prog-rockers' second Top Ten hit, "Come Sail Away," which reached Number Eight on the *Billboard* singles chart, and a Top 30 single in James Young's "Fooling Yourself." But the most dramatic track on the album, and one that was to become a firm fan favorite, was "Miss America," which continues the theme of combining the keyboard ethos of the progressive movement with the crunching guitar riffs of their more rock-orientated peers.

This is the first of Styx's albums to feature Tommy Shaw, replacing original guitarist John Curulewski. Throughout the album, it is Shaw's guitar work that shines, melding with that of founder member James Young, while Dennis DeYoung sings hysterical lyrics with a shrill confidence.

Number One singles:
None

Grammy Awards: None

Label: US & UK: A&M

Recorded in:
Chicago, USA

Personnel:
John Panozzo
Tommy Shaw
Dennis DeYoung
James "JY" Young
Chuck Panozzo

Producers:
Styx

1. **The Grand Illusion** (4:36)
2. **Fooling Yourself (The Angry Young Man)** (5:29)
3. **Superstars** (3:59)
4. **Come Sail Away** (6:07)
5. **Miss America** (5:01)
6. **Man in the Wilderness** (5:49)
7. **Castle Walls** (6:00)
8. **The Grand Finale** (1:58)

Total album length: 39 minutes

STYX

THE GRAND ILLUSION

82 Slowhand

| • **Album sales:** 3,100,000 | • **Release date:** November 1977 |

Eric Clapton's transformation from a 1960s guitar hero to a man at ease in the world of adult contemporary radio took shape on *Slowhand*, which found him and his band in a relaxed frame of mind.

Teaming up for the first time with producer Glyn Johns, whose past production and engineering credits had included The Beatles, The Rolling Stones, and The Who, this 1977 release was also a somewhat eclectic affair, absorbing blues, country, and mainstream rock.

Clapton's subdued approach is no more evident here than on "Wonderful Tonight," the first song he had prepared for the album and another tribute, after "Layla," to his future wife Patti Boyd, who had divorced George Harrison that year. Although quickly becoming a radio and slow-dance favorite, "Wonderful Tonight" only provided ammunition for critics to accuse Clapton of settling for lightweight, bland material.

But the album's opening cover of J.J. Cale's bluesy "Cocaine" set the right tone, while *Slowhand*'s tempo is taken up on the country-rock "Lay Down Sally," which became Clapton's biggest US hit since his 1974 cover of Bob Marley's "I Shot the Sheriff." The success of "Lay Down Sally" was also key to turning the album into Clapton's biggest seller to that point, with only the *Saturday Night Fever* soundtrack preventing it from taking the Number One position in the US.

Number one singles:
None

Grammy Awards: None

Label: US: RSO;
UK: Polydor

Recorded in: London, UK

Personnel:
Eric Clapton
Jamie Oldaker
Yvonne Elliman
Marcy Levy
Carl Radle
George Terry
Mel Collins
Dick Sims

Producer:
Glyn Johns

1. **Cocaine** (3:41)
2. **Wonderful Tonight** (3:44)
3. **Lay Down Sally** (3:56)
4. **Next Time You See Her** (4:01)
5. **We're All the Way** (2:32)
6. **The Core** (8:45)
7. **May You Never** (3:01)
8. **Mean Old Frisco** (4:42)
9. **Peaches and Diesel** (4:46)

Total album length: 39 minutes

ERIC CLAPTON
SLOWHAND

Sleeve artwork by Daniel Stewart and Watalu Asanuma

81 All 'N All

| • **Album sales:** 3,100,000 | • **Release date:** January 1978 |

The sudden death of Charles Stepney forced Earth, Wind & Fire's leader Maurice White into a rethink for the band's *All 'N All* album. In the absence of Stepney, who had arranged and co-produced all of the group's hit albums up to that point, White brought in long-time band associate Joe Wissert to co-produce the record, and started to look outside the Earth, Wind & Fire camp for assistance. This resulted in a first collaboration with up-and-coming arranger-producer David Foster.

Foster, who would later co-pen the Grammy-winning "After the Love Has Gone" for the band, was brought in as arranger for "Fantasy." Although only a modest crossover hit, "Fantasy" was an indication of where the group was now heading.

"Serpentine Fire" provided a third *Billboard* R&B Number One, as well as the ballad "I'll Write a Song for You." The fact that White wrote the album after a vacation in Brazil is evident on a series of interludes billed "Brazilian Rhyme," while the fusion of "Runnin'" was good enough to land the group a Best R&B Instrumental Grammy in January 1979, exactly a year after *All 'N All* peaked at Number Three on the US albums chart.

Number One singles:	**Producer:**
None	Maurice White

Grammy Awards:
Best R&B Vocal
Performance by a
Duo, Group, or Chorus;
Best R&B Instrumental
Performance: "Runnin'"

Label: US: Columbia;
UK: CBS

Recorded in: Los Angeles,
USA

Personnel:
Maurice White
Philip Bailey
Verdine White
Al McKay
Larry Dunn
Fred White
Ralph Johnson
Johnny Graham
Andrew Woolfolk
Don Myrick
Louis Sattefield

1. Serpentine Fire (3:50)
2. Fantasy (4:37)
3. In the Marketplace (interlude) (0:43)
4. Jupiter (3:11)
5. Love's Holiday (4:22)
6. Brazilian Rhyme (1:20)
7. I'll Write a Song for You (5:23)
8. Magic Wind (3:38)
9. Runnin' (5:50)
10. Brazilian Rhyme (interlude) (0:53)
11. Be Ever Wonderful (5:07)

Total album length: 39 minutes

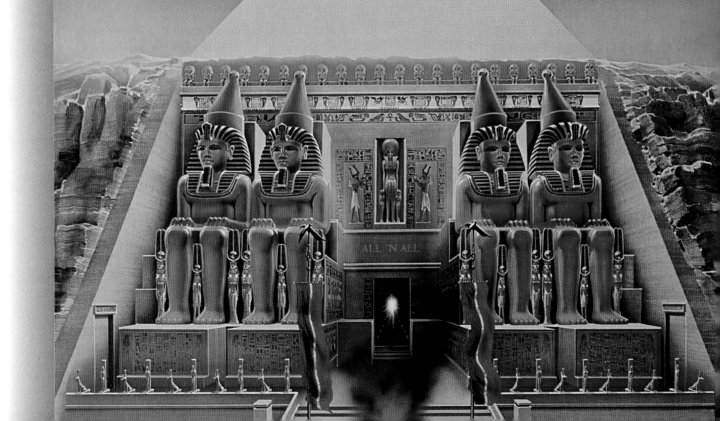

80 Sweet Baby James

| • **Album sales:** 3,150,000 | • **Release date:** March 1970 |

Featuring the US Top Three hit "Fire and Rain"—apparently as much about the suicide of a fellow patient during James Taylor's time in a psychiatric hospital as the love song it is often taken for—*Sweet Baby James* served to confirm the singer-songwriter's skills at weaving bittersweet country rock songs around love, friendship, loss, and life.

This, his second album, was full of the lilting introspection that had marked his eponymous debut set, recorded a year earlier for The Beatles' Apple label. Beautifully delivered, pared-back love songs include "Blossom"; there is country aplenty on the title track and "Anywhere Like Heaven"; and even a jazzed-up blues tune in "Steamroller," where Taylor is a "napalm bomb/guaranteed to blow your mind." With the US still embroiled in conflict in Vietnam and the hopes of the 1960s a fading memory, the album tapped into the prevailing post-hippie attitudes.

Sweet Baby James spent much of the 12 months following its release in the Top 10 of the US charts, and hit Number Seven in the UK. The success of the single and the album brought Taylor's first album and the single "Carolina on My Mind" back into the charts.

Number One singles:
None

Grammy Awards: None

Label: US & UK: Warner

Recorded in: Los Angeles, USA

Producer:
Peter Asher

Personnel:
James Taylor
Danny Kortchmar
Carole King
Russ Kunkel
Randy Meisner
Bobby West
John London
Red Rhodes
Jack Bielan
Chris Darrow

1. Sweet Baby James (2:54)
2. Lo and Behold (2:36)
3. Sunny Skies (2:21)
4. Steamroller (2:57)
5. Country Road (3:22)
6. Oh, Susannah (2:01)
7. Fire and Rain (3:24)
8. Blossom (2:14)
9. Anywhere Like Heaven (3:27)
10. Oh Baby, Don't You Loose Your Lip on Me (1:50)
11. Suite For 20G (4:41)

Total album length: 32 minutes

James Taylor

STEREO

WB
1843

JAMES TAYLOR
sweet baby james

79 Pearl

| • **Album sales:** 3,150,000 | • **Release date:** February 1971 |

*P*earl is widely acclaimed as Janis Joplin's greatest album, even though she succumbed to a heroin overdose before it was finished.

The 27-year-old had begun work on the album only a month earlier with her recently formed Full Tilt Boogie band when she was found dead on October 4, 1970, in a Hollywood motel. The recordings captured an artist at her full emotional powers, with her rasping voice backing her reputation as one of the finest white blues singers.

Released three months after Joplin's death, *Pearl* houses her most famous recording, a restrained yet heartbreaking cover of her one-time lover Kris Kristofferson's "Me and Bobby McGee." This became a posthumous Hot 100 Number One for Joplin in March 1971 as the album was in the midst of its own nine-week run at the top and a total of 42 weeks on the charts.

Joplin's reading of the soul ballad "A Woman Left Lonely" is harrowing, and a cover of the Garnett Mimms and The Enchanters' hit "Cry Baby" is chilling, but she allows for humor on "Mercedes Benz." One track, "Buried Alive in the Blues," is an instrumental, as she was scheduled to add vocals to it on the day after her death.

Pearl was chosen as the 122nd greatest album of all time by the editors of *Rolling Stone* magazine in 2003.

Number One singles:
US: "Me and Bobby McGee"

Grammy Awards: None

Label: US: Columbia; UK: CBS

Recorded in: Los Angeles, USA

Personnel:
Janis Joplin
Brad Campbell
John Till
Richard Bell
Ken Pearson
Clark Pierson

Producer:
Paul Rothchild

1. Move Over (3:43)
2. Cry Baby (3:58)
3. A Woman Left Lonely (3:29)
4. Half Moon (3:53)
5. Buried Alive in the Blues (2:27)
6. My Baby (3:45)
7. Me and Bobby McGee (4:31)
8. Mercedes Benz (1:47)
9. Trust Me (3:17)
10. Get It While You Can (3:33)

Total album length: 34 minutes

78 Teaser and the Firecat

| • **Album sales:** 3,150,000 | • **Release date:** September 1971 |

Complementing Cat Stevens's previous album, *Tea for the Tillerman*, and produced once again by Paul Samwell-Smith, *Teaser and the Firecat* blended a variety of styles—earnest folk-tinged ballads, up-tempo songs, light but far from frothy pop numbers, even traditional hymns—and consolidated the singer-songwriter's standing on both sides of the Atlantic.

The album spawned two hit singles in "Moonshadow" and Stevens' adaptation of the English hymn "Morning Has Broken," on which Rick Wakeman of Yes contributed the piano part. The song went on to chart at Number Nine in the UK and Number Six in the US.

In terms of chart positions, the album proved to be Stevens' most successful to date, reaching Number Three in the UK and Number Two in the US. A former art student, Stevens painted the album sleeve artwork.

Born to a Greek Cypriot father and Swedish mother in London, in 1977 Stevens converted to Islam, changed his name to Yusuf Islam, and dissociated himself from his pop music. He invested the royalties from his records in Muslim schools and charities. It was to be 25 years before Stevens began recording and performing pop music again.

Number One singles:
None

Grammy Awards: None

Label: US: A&M;
UK: Island

Recorded in: N/A

Producer:
Paul Samwell-Smith

Personnel:
Cat Stevens
Alun Davies
Larry Steele
Gerry Conway
Harvey Burns
Rick Wakeman
Andreas Toumazis
Angelos Hatzipavli
Del Newman

1. The Wind (1:42)
2. Rubylove (2:37)
3. If I Laugh (3:20)
4. Changes IV (3:32)
5. How Can I Tell You (4:27)
6. Tuesday's Dead (3:36)
7. Morning Has Broken (3:20)
8. Bitterblue (3:12)
9. Moonshadow (2:52)
10. Peace Train (4:11)

Total album length: 33 minutes

CAT STEVENS

77 Goat's Head Soup

• Album sales: 3,150,000 | **• Release date:** September 1973 |

There are those who suggest that The Rolling Stones are going through the motions on *Goat's Head Soup*. Whatever the album's weaknesses, perceived or otherwise, it is still a "typical" Stones record, albeit less frenetic and angry, and more thoughtful and measured, than earlier work.

Critics at the time said that *Goat's Head Soup* didn't stand out from the rest of the releases of the day in the way a Stones album normally would. True enough, there are few really remarkable tracks aside from the lilting "Angie," one of their greatest songs and one that remains in their live sets today.

Recorded at Dynamic Studios, in Kingston, Jamaica, the making of the record was not helped by another legal battle over drugs, this one dating back to their stay in France when they were recording *Exile on Main Street*. Occasional funk breaks are provided once again by keyboardist Billy Preston, while Nicky Hopkins contributes piano on "Angie" and some other tracks.

The band's fanbase appears not to have heeded the critics' downbeat assessment of the record, and it topped the album charts on both sides of the Atlantic soon after its release in the fall of 1973. "Angie" reached Number One in the US and Number Five in the UK.

Number One singles:
US: "Angie"

Grammy Awards: None

Label: US & UK: Rolling Stones

Recorded in: Kingston, Jamaica

Personnel:
Mick Jagger
Keith Richards
Mick Taylor
Bill Wyman
Charlie Watts
Billy Preston
Nicky Hopkins

Producer:
Jimmy Miller

1. Dancing With Mr. D. (4:53)
2. 100 Years Ago (3:59)
3. Coming Down Again (5:55)
4. Doo Doo Doo Doo Doo (Heartbreaker) (3:27)
5. Angie (4:33)
6. Silver Train (4:26)
7. Hide Your Love (4:12)
8. Winter (5:30)
9. Can You Hear the Music (5:32)
10. Star Star (4:25)

Total album length: 47 minutes

The Rolling Stones

76 Back Home Again

| • **Album sales:** 3,150,000 | • **Release date:** August 1974 |

John Denver took his friendly, narrative songwriting a step further with *Back Home Again*. Featuring a cover shot of Denver and wife Annie—hence "Annie's Song"—the album found the singer at his most uplifting and generous of spirit; indeed, Denver was the commercial antidote for those who found the visions of Neil Young or Bob Dylan too demanding. The album features some of Denver's best-loved songs, including "On the Road," the tale of a young boy experiencing love at first sight while on a car journey with his father, and "Matthew," written as a memorial to his uncle, Dean Deutschendorf, who died in car accident, aged 21.

The album's highlight is the phenomenally successful "Annie's Song," which brought Denver not only domestic success but also international acclaim in various guises, including flautist James Galway's UK instrumental hit single. The album topped the US and UK charts.

This is not music to challenge, more to comfort, and the platinum status of the album—with similar awards for "Annie's Song," "Thank God I'm a Country Boy," and the title track—shows just how faithfully Denver was able to chime with his audience.

Number One singles:
US & UK: "Annie's Song"

Grammy Awards: None

Label: US & UK: RCA Victor

Recorded in: N/A

Producer:
Milton Okun

Personnel:
John Denver
John Sommers
Dick Kniss
Eric Weissberg
Jim Gordon
Hal Blaine
Jim Connor
Julie Connor
Glen D. Hardin
Lee Holdridge
David Jackson
Richard Kniss
Buddy Collette
Steve Weisberg

1. Back Home Again (4:42)
2. On the Road (2:33)
3. Grandma's Feather Bed (2:15)
4. Matthew (3:43)
5. Thank God I'm a Country Boy (3:06)
6. Music is You (1:26)
7. Annie's Song (2:58)
8. It's Up To You (2:26)
9. Cool an' Green an' Shady (3:07)
10. Eclipse (3:41)
11. Sweet Surrender (5:29)
12. This Old Guitar (2:50)

Total album length: 38 minutes

Captain Fantastic and the Brown Dirt Cowboy

| • **Album sales:** 3,150,000 | • **Release date:** May 1975 |

Elton John and Bernie Taupin (John's lyricist) turned inward for 1975's *Captain Fantastic and the Brown Dirt Cowboy* to take stock of their incredible rise from struggling songwriters to international stardom.

The first album ever to debut at the top of the US album chart, *Captain Fantastic* came amid a torturous time for the singer, who, while arguably then the most famous musical star on the planet, was fighting depression and chemical dependency. Its highly personal theme is illustrated by the set's best-known cut and Top Four US hit, the hauntingly beautiful "Someone Saved My Life Tonight," apparently inspired by a suicide attempt by the artist while he was living with a girlfriend who hated his music.

Written on a cruise liner, the album was the second following 1974's disappointing *Caribou* to be recorded at the Caribou ranch in Colorado. It was John's first new studio release in nearly a year after a prolific period in which he had put out six all-new sets in little more than three years.

Although a commercial triumph, it is a more subtle affair than its predecessors; it follows a distinct theme rather than comprising one potential hit single after another. The album managed seven weeks at Number One in the US—it peaked at Number Two in the UK—and marked a creative peak for the two songwriters, although a decline set in from then on.

Number One singles:
None

Grammy Awards: None

Label: US: MCA;
UK: DJM.

Recorded in:
Colorado, USA

Personnel:
Elton John
Dee Murray
Davey Johnstone
Ray Cooper
Nigel Olsson

Producer:
Gus Dudgeon

1. Captain Fantastic and the Brown Dirt Cowboy (5:46)
2. Tower of Babel (4:28)
3. Bitter Fingers (4:33)
4. Tell Me When the Whistle Blows (4:20)
5. Someone Saved My Life Tonight (6:44)
6. (Gotta Get a) Meal Ticket (4:01)
7. Better Off Dead (2:37)
8. Writing (3:40)
9. We All Fall in Love Sometimes (4:12)
10. Curtains (6:34)

Total album length: 47 minutes

74 One More From the Road

| • **Album sales:** 3,150,000 | • **Release date:** October 1976 |

"What song is it you wanna hear?" is perhaps one of the most famous introductions to a song on a live album. Ronnie Van Zandt's question, posed to the thousands packed into Atlanta's Fox Theater on a hot July night in 1976, elicited the massive response "Free Bird!!!," Skynyrd's anthem.

The Southern-influenced rock of Lynyrd Skynyrd had touched fans throughout the US, a popularity captured on this concert album. From Van Zandt's gritty vocals to the guitar duels of Gary Rossington and Allen Collins, Skynyrd were in their element. *One More From the Road* reached Number Nine in the US and Number 17 in the UK. Songs such as "Sweet Home Alabama," with its by now infamous swipe at Neil Young, through to "Gimme Back My Bullets" and the achingly sweet ballad "Tuesday's Gone" show the range of the band and what might follow in the years to come.

Sadly, it was not to be. A little over a year after the album was released to huge critical and commercial acclaim, Van Zandt, Steven Gaines, Gaines's sister Cassie, and road manager Dean Kilpatrick were killed in a plane crash while the band were on tour.

Number One singles:
None

Grammy Awards: None

Label: US & UK: MCA

Recorded in: Atlanta, Georgia, USA

Producer:
Tom Dowd

Personnel:
Ronnie Van Zandt
Allen Collins
Gary Rossington
Billy Powell
Leon Wilkinson
Artimus Pyle
Steven Gaines
Cassie Gaines
Jo Billingsley
Leslie Hawkins

1. Workin For MCA (5:32)
2. I Ain't the One (3:47)
3. Saturday Night Special (5:39)
4. Searching (4:00)
5. Travelin' Man (4:37)
6. Simple Man (6:56)
7. Whiskey Rock a Roller (4:48)
8. The Needle and the Spoon (4:35)
9. Gimme Back My Bullets (4:01)
10. Tuesday's Gone (8:25)
11. Gimme Three Steps (5:11)
12. Call Me the Breeze (5:50)
13. T For Texas (9:14)
14. Sweet Home Alabama (7:29)
15. Crossroads (4:16)
16. Free Bird (14:25)

Total album length:
1 hour 38 minutes

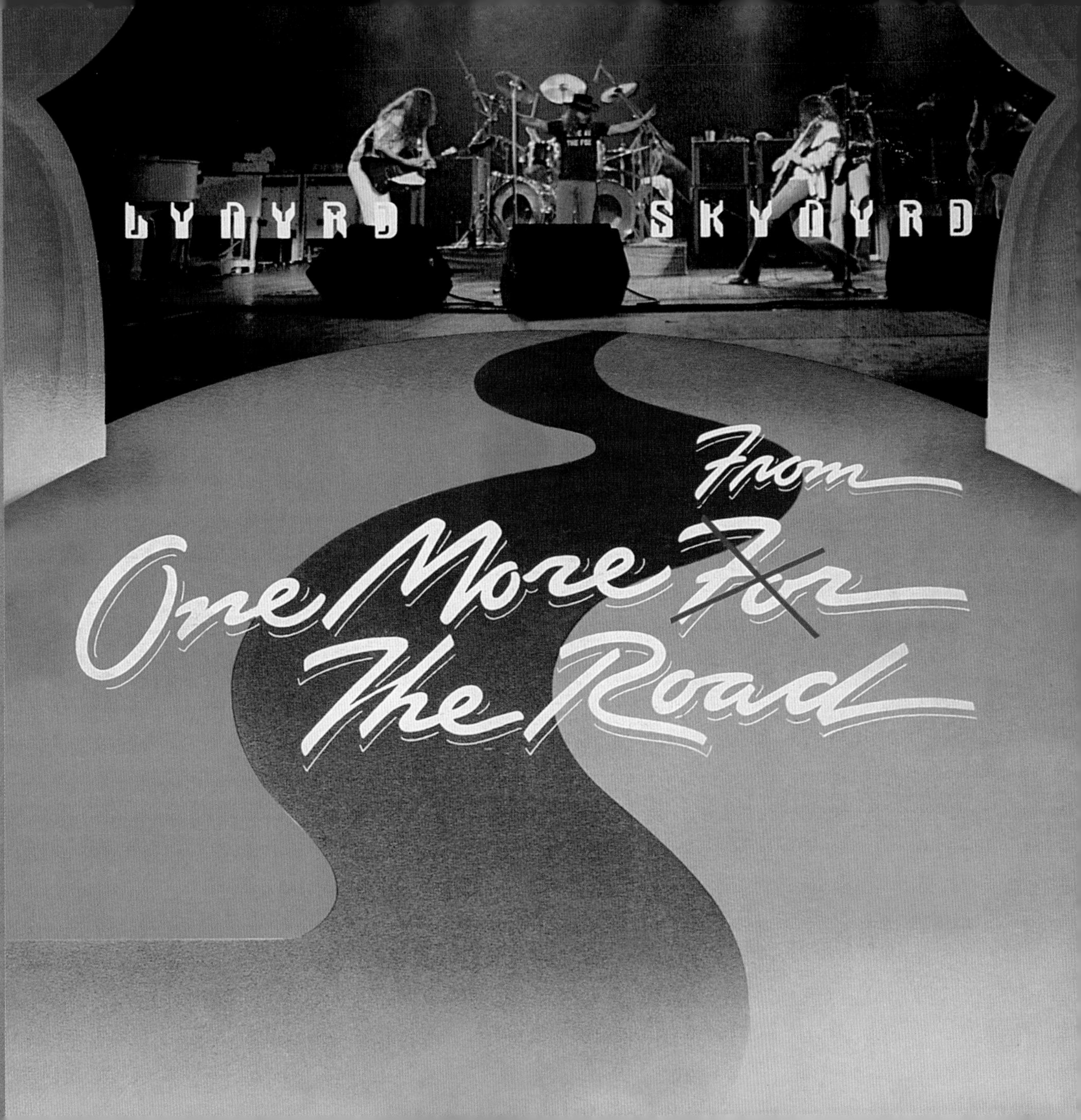
LYNYRD SKYNYRD
From
One More For
The Road

73 Tubular Bells

• **Album sales:** 3,250,000 | • **Release date:** May 1973

Mike Oldfield's debut, recorded when he was just 19, remains his biggest-selling and most famous work. Something of a musical prodigy, English multi-instrumentalist Oldfield had been playing guitar and bass professionally since he was 17, but record labels kept turning down his demos because they couldn't see the commercial potential in a pop album that largely lacked any vocals.

In time, though, Oldfield was signed by entrepreneur Richard Branson, and *Tubular Bells* became the first album released by Branson's Virgin Records.

Repeatedly overdubbing, Oldfield played almost all the instruments himself. Not only are the vocals very much secondary, the whole album consists of just two lengthy instrumental tracks—one for each side of the record.

Sales were modest at first, but were given a massive boost after the opening music was featured—albeit only in two scenes—in the movie *The Exorcist*, released in the US in December 1973 and the UK the following spring. Following that, the album topped the charts in the UK and reached Number Three in the US *Billboard* 200.

In subsequent years, Oldfield continued to make progressive rock, as well as branching out into mainstream pop songwriting, movie scores, and, in the 1990s, returning to record *Tubular Bells II* and *Tubular Bells III*.

Number One singles:
None

Grammy Awards:
Best Instrumental
Composition

Label: Virgin

Recorded in:
The Manor, Oxfordshire,
England

Personnel:
Mike Oldfield
Steve Broughton
Lindsay L. Cooper
Jon Field
Mundy Ellis
Sally Oldfield
Vivian Stanshall

Producers:
Tom Newman
Simon Heyworth
Mike Oldfield

1. **Tubular Bells, Part One (25:30)**
2. **Tubular Bells, Part Two (23:20)**

Total album length: 48 minutes

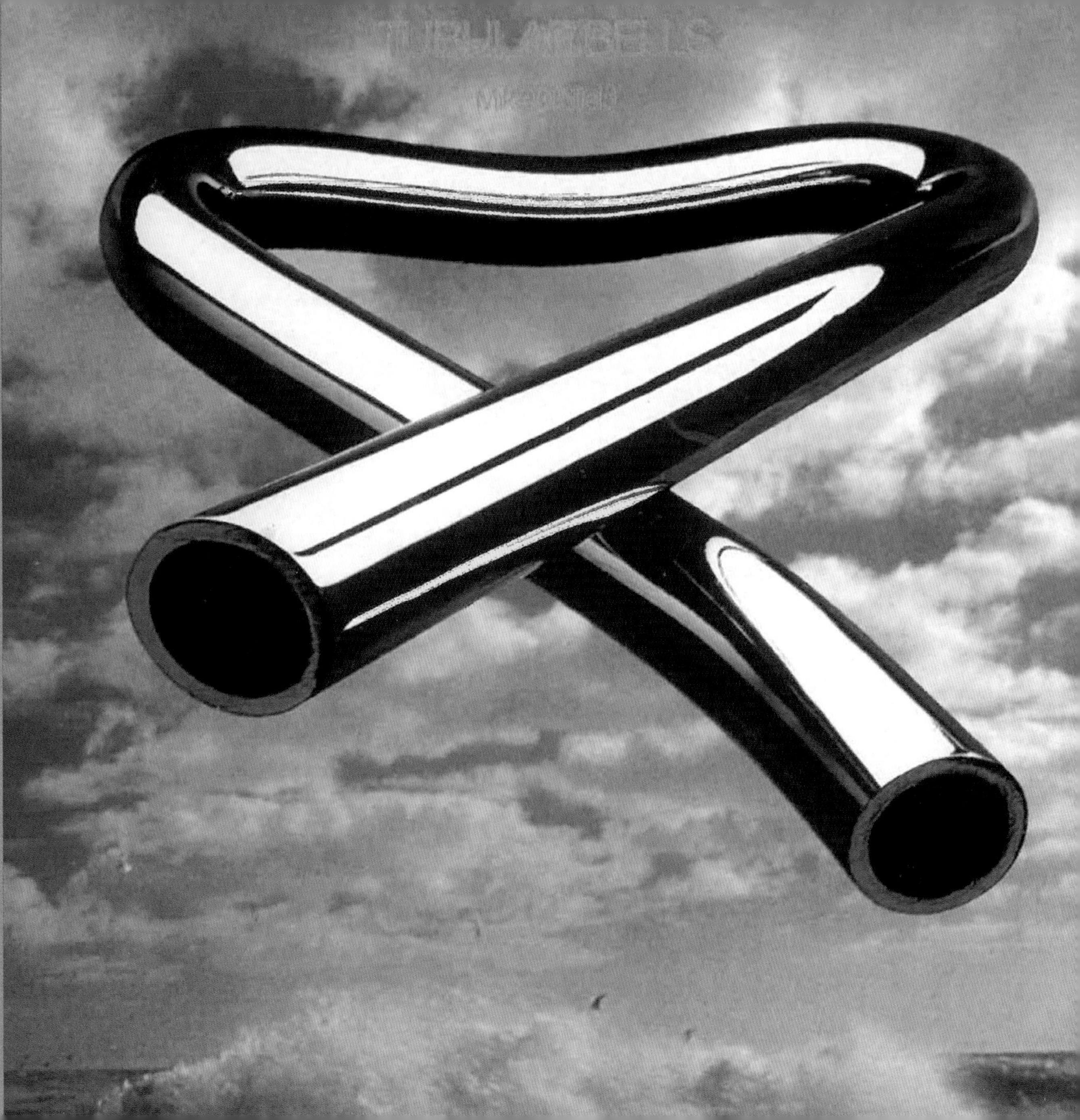

Sleeve artwork by Trevor Key

Tea for the Tillerman

| • **Album sales:** 3,300,000 | • **Release date:** November 1970 |

Tea for the Tillerman built on the early promise of Cat Stevens's comeback album, *Mona Bone Jakon*, and established the English singer-songwriter as a major talent in America.

With his career having been on pause at the end of the 1960s after contracting tuberculosis, Stevens re-emerged with perfect timing early the following decade, just as the singer-songwriter movement was taking hold.

Opening track "Where Do the Children Play?" typified Stevens's new direction. A seemingly straightforward pop song, on closer examination it addressed the artist's concerns about the price society was paying for the advancement of technology. "Wild World," his first US Top 20 single (Number 11), provided a novel twist on

the breakup song, while "Father and Son" cast its writer in both title parts in a conversation between the generations.

Ex-Yardbird Paul Samwell-Smith provided a loose, gentle production, which allowed Stevens's songs to breathe. Urged on by the success of "Wild World," the album took five months after its release to reach a peak of Number Eight in America, where it stayed on the chart for 79 weeks; in the UK, it reached a more modest Number 20.

Songs from this album have been recorded by a diverse range of artists, from Jimmy Cliff, Mr Big, and Maxi Priest ("Wild World") to Boyzone ("Father and Son").

Number One singles:
None

Grammy Awards: None

Label: US: A&M;
UK: Island

Recorded in: N/A

Personnel:
Cat Stevens
Alun Davies
John Ryan
Harvey Burns
John Rostein
Del Newman

Producer:
Paul Samwell-Smith

1. Where Do the Children Play? (3:52)
2. Hard Headed Woman (3:47)
3. Wild World (3:20)
4. Sad Lisa (3:45)
5. Miles From Nowhere (3:37)
6. But I Might Die Tonight (1:53)
7. Longer Boats (3:12)
8. Into White (3:24)
9. On the Road To Find Out (5:08)
10. Father and Son (3:41)
11. Tea for the Tillerman (1:01)

Total album length: 37 minutes

Cat Stevens

Tea for the Tillerman
CAT STEVENS

71 Aqualung

| • **Album sales:** 3,300,000 | • **Release date:** May 1971 |

The weighty subject matter of its contents proved no barrier to *Aqualung* becoming the album that turned American radio on to Jethro Tull. Despite the prog rockers' leader Ian Anderson using this 1971 release to explore the deep themes of humanity's relationship with God, the music here was compelling enough to elevate several of the cuts into FM staples and send Jethro Tull into the US Top 10 for the first time.

According to Anderson, the album is not a concept album but "a bunch of songs"; nevertheless, *Aqualung* is basically divided into two themes, with its original A-side about a lecherous character called Aqualung and the flip side a rebuke on organized religion.

Aqualung is notable for the performance of guitarist Martin Barre, whose playing on the likes of the title track, "My God," and "Locomotive Breath" turned them into classic rock songs. Another radio favorite, "Cross-Eyed Mary," highlights Tull's trademark flute-over-drums sound.

Recorded after original bass player Jeffrey Hammond-Hammond returned to the lineup to replace the departing Glenn Cornick, the album reached Number Four in the UK and hit a US chart peak of Number Seven in June 1971, spending 76 weeks on the charts.

Number One singles:
None

Grammy Awards: None

Label: US: Reprise;
UK: Chrysalis

Recorded in: London, UK

Personnel:
Ian Anderson
Martin Barre
Clive Bunker
John Evans
Jeffrey Hammond-
    Hammond

Producers:
Ian Anderson
Terry Ellis

1. Aqualung (6:31)
2. Cross-Eyed Mary (4:06)
3. Cheap Day Return (1:21)
4. Mother Goose (3:51)
5. Wond'ring Aloud (1:53)
6. Up To Me (3:14)
7. My God (7:08)
8. Hymn 43 (3:15)
9. Slipstream (1:12)
10. Locomotive Breath (4:23)
11. Wind Up (6:01)

Total album length: 43 minutes

70 Darkness on the Edge of Town

| • **Album sales:** 3,300,000 | • **Release date:** June 1978 |

A near three-year gap separates *Darkness on the Edge of Town* from its predecessor, the star-confirming *Born To Run*, a delay caused by Bruce Springsteen's acrimonious lawsuit with his former manager. In that time, the songwriter had clearly lost none of his energy and ability to encapsulate the American blue-collar experience.

Eleven months in the making, sales for the new album did not match *Born To Run's* six million; however, it managed Number Five on the Hot 100 chart in the US, while actually bettering its predecessor's showing in the UK, peaking at Number 16.

Darkness on the Edge of Town was intended to be a sparser record than *Born To Run*, but it sounds just as powerful. "I just had a specific thing in mind," the singer explained later; "it had to be relentless."

A great deal has been made of the creative influence wielded by producer—and later manager—Jon Landau, who is said to have guided the singer-songwriter back toward a more stripped-down sound, with songs averaging four minutes in length. Certainly, the album's overall brevity is a new departure, although the almost seven-minute "Racing In the Street" was a portent of things to come on Springsteen's follow-up, *The River*, a double album lasting 83 minutes.

Number One singles:
None

Grammy Awards: None

Label: US: Columbia;
UK: CBS.

Recorded in: New York,
USA

Personnel:
Bruce Springsteen
Clarence Clemons
Stevie van Zandt
Danny Federici
Roy Bittan
Garry Talent
Max Weinburg

Producers:
Jon Landau
Bruce Springsteen

1. Badlands (4:04)
2. Adam Raised a Cain (4:34)
3. Something in the Night (5:14)
4. Candy's Room (2:48)
5. Racing in the Street (6:54)
6. The Promised Land (4:29)
7. Factory (2:19)
8. Streets of Fire (4:03)
9. Prove it All Night (4:01)
10. Darkness on the Edge of Town (4:29)

Total album length: 43 minutes

Bruce
Springsteen
Darkness
on the Edge
of Town

69 Band on the Run

| • **Album sales:** 3,350,000 | • **Release date:** December 1973 |

Paul McCartney's post-Beatles output reached a critical and commercial peak on *Band on the Run*, which brought him to the closest point of reaching the quality threshold of his Fab Four days. His fifth album since quitting The Beatles just three years earlier, this 1973 release avoids the lightweight pitfalls of many of McCartney's solo projects, capturing instead a reinvigorated artist confident in his abilities once more.

Mostly created in Lagos, Nigeria, the album's success came despite not only two members of his band, Wings, quitting on the eve of recording, but also Paul and his wife Linda being robbed at knifepoint of their possessions, including the album's demos.

The departures left a tight nucleus of the McCartneys and Denny Laine, with Beatles veteran Geoff Emerick engineering and other musicians drafted in where needed. McCartney also called upon a series of famous associates for the front cover shot, including the likes of movie star James Coburn and actor Christopher Lee dressed as convicts.

Topping both the UK and US chart in the spring of 1974, the album's many highlights include the complexly structured title track, a US chart-topper in its own right in June 1974, the powerful "Jet," and the laidback "Let Me Roll It." "Helen Wheels," which reached Number 10 on the singles charts, was inspired by McCartney's nickname for his Land Rover.

Number One singles:
US: "Band on the Run"

Grammy Awards:
Best Pop Vocal Performance by a Duo, Group, or Chorus; Best Engineered Recording

Label: US & UK: Apple

Recorded in: Lagos, Nigeria & London, UK

Personnel:
Paul McCartney
Linda McCartney
Denny Laine
Various others

Producer:
Paul McCartney

1. Band on the Run (5:13)
2. Jet (4:09)
3. Bluebird (3:24)
4. Mrs Vandebilt (4:42)
5. Let Me Roll It (4:50)
6. Mamunia (4:50)
7. No Words (2:34)
8. Helen Wheels (3:48)
9. Picasso's Last Words (Drink To Me) (5:49)
10. Nineteen Hundred and Eighty Five (5:29)

Total album length: 45 minutes

68 Presence

• **Album sales:** 3,350,000 │ • **Release date:** March 1976

A Number One on the UK album charts and the US *Billboard* Top 200, Led Zeppelin's seventh studio album was prompted after the band had to cancel a tour following Robert Plant's injury in a car crash. During Plant's convalescence, he and Jimmy Page worked on the lyrics and the music, before being joined by the rest of the band in Munich to record the album.

Following a month of rehearsals, the album was recorded in just 18 days, with Plant performing all his vocals while in a wheelchair.

Unlike their previous release, 1975's *Physical Graffiti*, *Presence* was a straightforward hard rock album, with barely any acoustic guitar, ballads, or intricate arrangements.

Although selling well, the album received a mixed reception from critics. Only two of the tracks, "Achilles Last Stand" and "Nobody's Fault but Mine," ever made it on to the Led Zeppelin live set list before John Bonham's death in 1980. Hipgnosis's album cover, with a family seated around a small obelisk, is, according to Jimmy Page, "Sort of a joke on the film *2001*."

Number One singles:
None

Grammy Awards: None

Label: Swan Song

Recorded in: Munich, Germany

Personnel:
Robert Plant
Jimmy Page
John Paul Jones
John Bonham

Producer:
Jimmy Page

1. **Achilles Last Stand** (10:30)
2. **For Your Life** (6:21)
3. **Royal Orleans** (2:59)
4. **Nobody's Fault but Mine** (6:16)
5. **Candy Store Rock** (4:08)
6. **Hots on for Nowhere** (4:44)
7. **Tea for One** (9.23)

Total album length: 31 minutes

Led Zeppelin

67 Foot Loose & Fancy Free

| • **Album sales:** 3,350,000 | • **Release date:** November 1977 |

During a highly successful career with UK rock outfit The Faces, frontman Rod Stewart also plowed a solo furrow. Once the band folded in the early 1970s, he set about pursuing his ambitions in the US.

Recorded at the Manta Sound Studio in Toronto, Canada, *Foot Loose & Fancy Free* taps into both Stewart's musical heritage of balladeering and boogie-blues, as on opener "Hot Legs," along with the then-current craze for all things disco.

Ballads include the excellent "I Was Only Joking" and "You Got a Nerve," both cowritten by Stewart and guitarist Gary Grainger. "You're

In My Heart" was a Number Three hit in the UK, reaching Number Four in the US.

Unfortunately, Stewart does little justice to the Holland/Dozier/Holland classic "You Keep Me Hangin' On," surely a case where the composers were happier with the royalty check than the rendition that appeared on the album.

Foot Loose & Fancy Free narrowly missed out on a top album slot in the US, managing to reach Number Two on the Hot 100, while in the UK it peaked at Number Three. Disco would show an even greater influence on Stewart's follow-up album, *Blondes Have More Fun*.

Number One singles:
None

Grammy Awards: None

Label: US: Warners;
UK: Riva

Recorded in: Toronto,
Canada

Personnel:
Rod Stewart
Jim Cregan
Gary Grainger
Steve Cropper
Billy Peek
Fred Tackett
Phil Chen
Carmine Appice

Producer:
Tom Dowd

1. **Hot Legs** (5:14)
2. **You're Insane** (4:51)
3. **You're In My Heart (The Final Acclaim)** (4:30)
4. **Born Loose** (6:04)
5. **You Keep Me Hangin' On** (7:28)
6. **(If Loving You Is Wrong) I Don't Want To Be Right** (5:26)
7. **You Got a Nerve** (4:59)
8. **I Was Only Joking** (6:07)

Total album length: 44 minutes

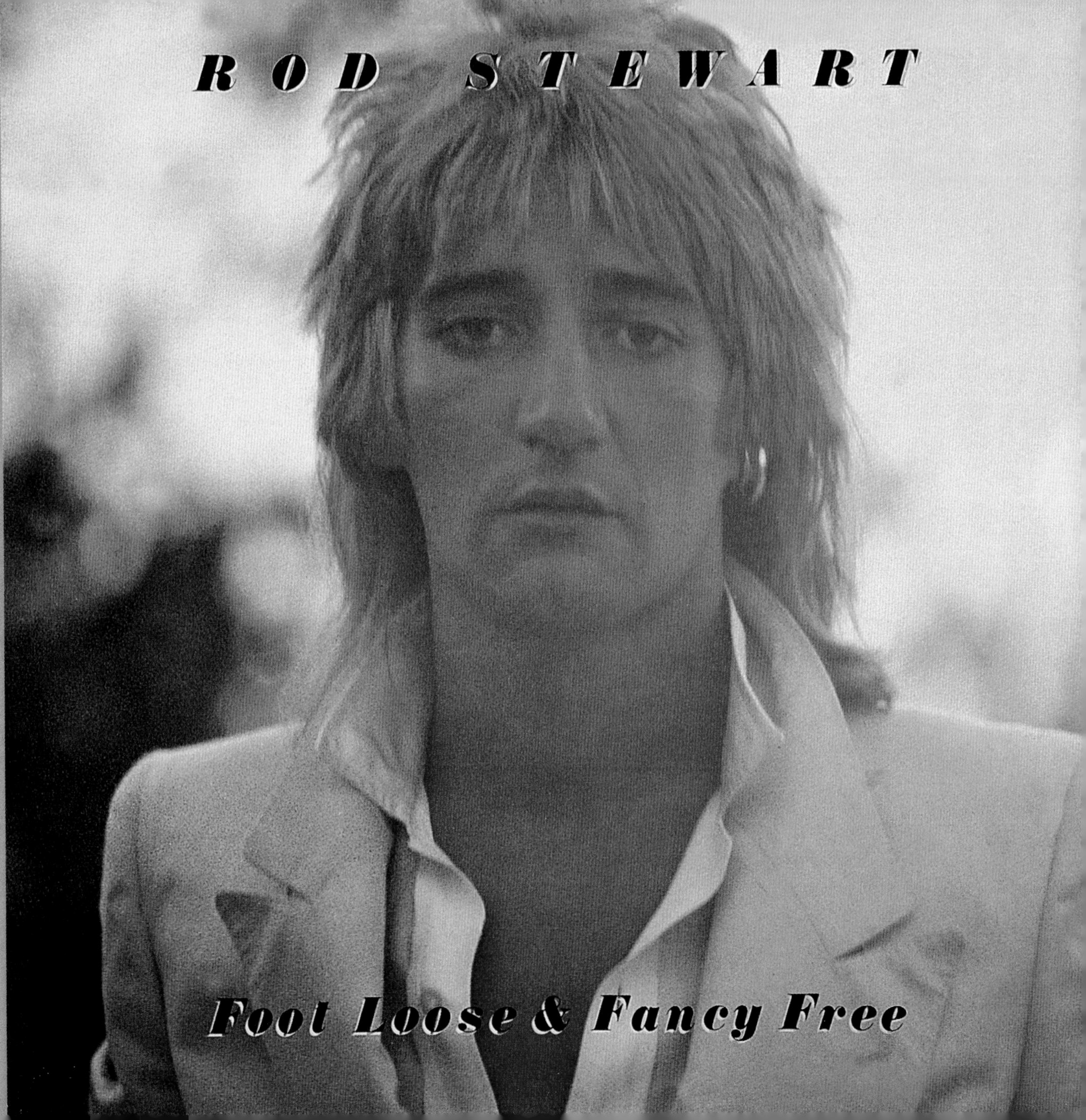

ROD STEWART

Foot Loose & Fancy Free

66 Sticky Fingers

| • **Album sales:** 3,400,000 | • **Release date:** April 1971 |

The raw energy of *Sticky Fingers* is for many the highpoint of The Rolling Stones' career. From the opening blast of "Brown Sugar" through to the plaintive "Can't You Hear Me Knocking" and then into typical Stones territory on "Bitch," with its brassy, raunchy refrain, the album assaults the senses.

Even when the pace does ease, as on the classic ballad "Wild Horses," the Marianne Faithfull co-penned "Sister Morphine," and "Moonlight Mile," the sense of dark foreboding remains.

In addition to the beautiful country rock of "Dead Flowers," the band's love affair with the blues is illustrated by their version of McDowell/Davis's "You Gotta Move" and Jagger/Richards'

"I Got the Blues." The album was the third to feature ex-John Mayall's Bluesbreakers' guitarist Mick Taylor, who had been recruited following Brian Jones' accidental death in 1969.

Jagger's "Brown Sugar," a song variously interpreted to be about heroin, interracial sex, or slavery—or all three—reached Number One in the US and Number Two in the UK. "Wild Horses" peaked at Number 28 in the US.

Sticky Fingers, the first Stones album to be released on their own Rolling Stones label, topped the album charts in both the US and the UK. The original album sleeve, designed by Andy Warhol and featuring a male crotch with a working zipper, was banned in Spain.

Number One singles:
US: "Brown Sugar"

Grammy Awards: None

Label: US & UK: Rolling Stones

Recorded in: London, UK

Personnel:
Mick Jagger
Keith Richards
Mick Taylor
Bill Wyman
Charlie Watts
Bobby Keys

Producer:
Jimmy Miller

1. Brown Sugar (3:49)
2. Sway (3:52)
3. Wild Horses (5:44)
4. Can't You Hear Me Knocking (7:15)
5. You Gotta Move (2:34)
6. Bitch (3:37)
7. I Got the Blues (3:54)
8. Sister Morphine (5:34)
9. Dead Flowers (4:05)
10. Moonlight Mile (5:56)

Total album length: 46 minutes

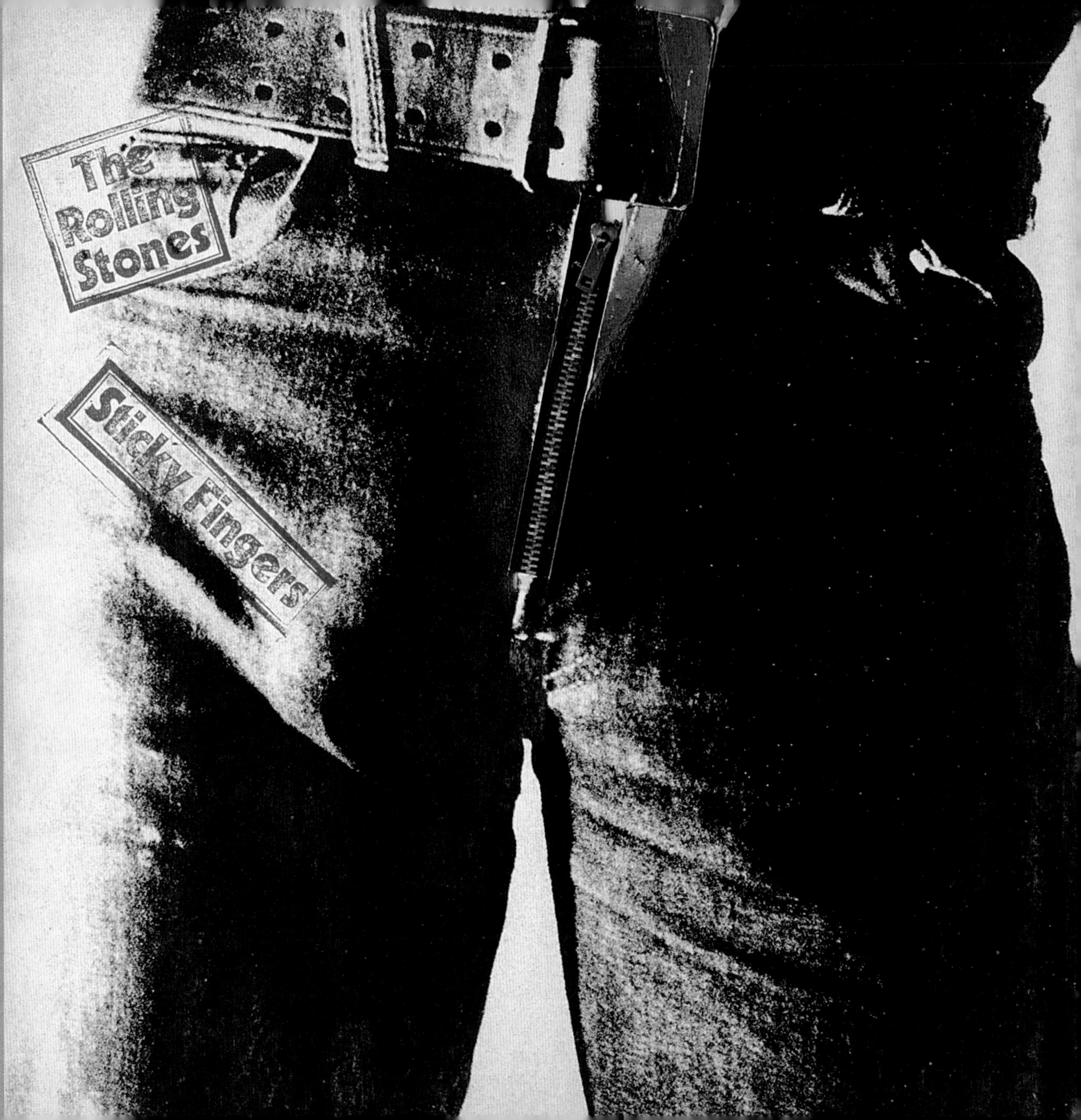

Sleeve artwork by Craig Braun and Andy Warhol

65 A Night at the Opera

| • **Album sales:** 3,400,000 | • **Release date:** December 1975 |

A *Night at the Opera*, Queen's fourth album, firmly established the band in the hearts and minds of US music consumers, while it merely served to confirm their status as one of the most popular rock acts in their native UK. The album scored a Number Nine position in the US, bettering its predecessor, *Sheer Heart Attack*, by three places, while in the UK the album was the band's first chart-topper.

The song for which Queen is best known, "Bohemian Rhapsody," was arguably the first track to benefit from having a video. This epic spent nine weeks at the UK Number One across Christmas 1975 (selling 1.19 million), though only reaching Number Nine in the US. It returned to the top of the UK charts for a further five weeks at Christmas 1991, a few weeks after the death of lead singer, Freddie Mercury, making it the seventh-best-selling single ever at the time.

Mercury and guitarist Brian May shouldered most of the album's songwriting duties: "Bohemian Rhapsody" was penned by Mercury, as was the vaudevillian "Seaside Rendezvous," while most of the rest, including the Buffalo Springfield-esque "'39" and out-and-out rocker "Sweet Lady," were composed by May. Yet bassist John Deacon contributes to great effect with the delightfully simple love song "You're My Best Friend," which reached Number Seven on the UK singles chart and Number 16 on the US.

Number One singles: UK: "Bohemian Rhapsody"

Grammy Awards: None

Label: US: Elektra; UK: EMI

Recorded in: Various locations, UK

Personnel:
Freddie Mercury
Brian May
John Deacon
Roger Taylor

Producers:
Roy Thomas Baker
Queen

1. Death on Two Legs (3:43)
2. Lazing on a Sunday Afternoon (1:07)
3. I'm in Love With My Car (3:05)
4. You're My Best Friend (2:52)
5. '39 (3:31)
6. Sweet Lady (4:04)
7. Seaside Rendezvous (2:16)
8. The Prophet's Song (8:21)
9. Love of My Life (3:39)
10. Good Company (3:23)
11. Bohemian Rhapsody (5:55)
12. God Save the Queen (1:15)

Total album length: 43 minutes

Queen

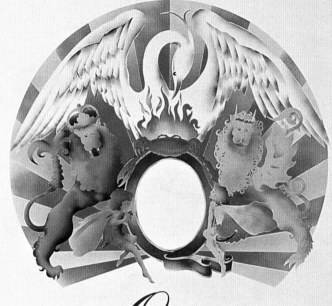

64 | Who's Next

| • **Album sales:** 3,550,000 | • **Release date:** August 1971 |

Although it was originally intended as part of a multimedia conceptual project spearheaded by guitarist and Who lynchpin Pete Townshend (the accompanying screenplay about an apocalyptic world never come to fruition), *Who's Next* seems a remarkably straightforward rock record when compared to the grandiose musical wanderings of the band's previous studio album, the rock opera *Tommy*.

Over the years, the album has come to be regarded as one of the band's most respected works. In 1987, a panel of rock critics and broadcasters brought together by *Rolling Stone* magazine placed *Who's Next* in their top 20 rock albums of all time. It has also proved to be The Who's most commercially successful record, reaching Number One in the UK album charts and Number Four in the US, where it spent 41 weeks on the charts.

Who's Next was first showcased informally, with the band playing material at London's Young Vic Theatre on three consecutive Mondays during the spring of 1971. Among the tracks are three of the band's most popular songs: "Baba O'Riley," with its looped synthesizer riff (Townshend was one of the first musicians to use synthesizers and samples in rock), the multilayered and subversive "Behind Blue Eyes," and what was to become another long-lived concert staple, "Won't Get Fooled Again." For anyone doubting The Who's ability to come up with a subtle, lovelorn tune, there is also "The Song is Over."

Number One singles:
None

Grammy Awards: None

Label: US: Decca;
UK: Track

Recorded in: Various
locations, UK

Personnel:
Roger Daltrey
Pete Townshend
John Entwhistle
Keith Moon

Producers:
The Who
Glyn Johns

1. **Baba O'Riley** (5:09)
2. **Bargain** (5:34)
3. **Love Ain't For Keeping** (2:10)
4. **My Wife** (3:41)
5. **The Song is Over** (6:14)
6. **Getting in Tune** (4:50)
7. **Going Mobile** (3:43)
8. **Behind Blue Eyes** (3:42)
9. **Won't Get Fooled Again** (8:33)

Total album length: 39 minutes

The Who

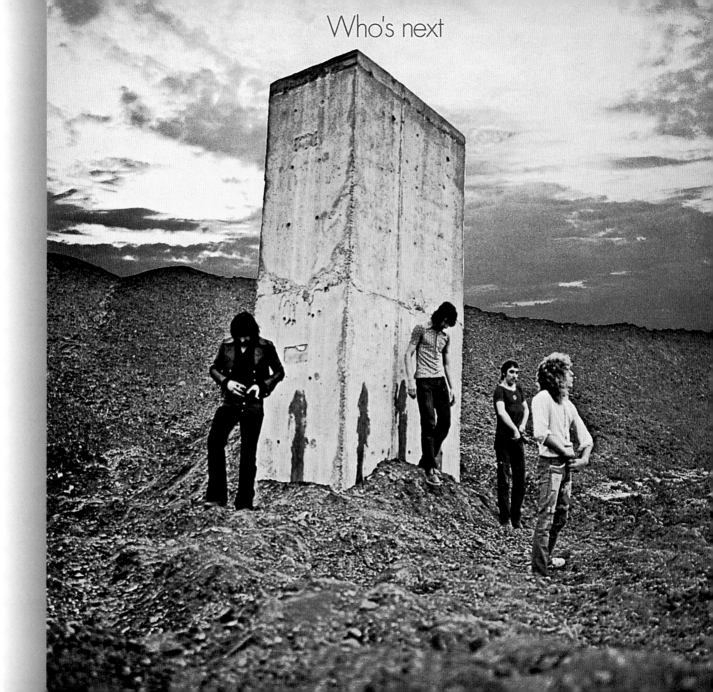

63 Blondes Have More Fun

| • **Album sales:** 4,050,000 | • **Release date:** December 1978 |

There are those who believe that Rod Stewart lost the plot when he moved to America and left behind his harder, bluesier-edged sound. Nevertheless, his late 1970s work—and *Blondes Have More Fun* in particular—has proved to be the peak of his commercial success.

The album's lead single, "Do Ya Think I'm Sexy?," was seen by many as a blatant ploy by Stewart to hitch his star to the disco wave. No matter; with a pulsing bass line and irreverent lyrics, it worked like a charm. The song topped the singles charts in both the US and the UK, selling 250,000 copies a week in February 1979, when it made Number One. It was the fastest-selling single in Warners' history and their first platinum single of the year. The track also topped the charts in 11 countries, including France, Germany, Holland, Sweden, Norway, Italy, Belgium, Australia, and Canada. Stewart donated all his publishing royalties from the song to UNICEF.

The follow-up single, the melodic strum-along "Ain't Love a Bitch," managed Numbers 11 and 22 in the UK and US respectively. The album itself reached Number One in the US and Number Three in the UK.

Number One singles:
US & UK: "Do Ya Think I'm Sexy?"

Grammy Awards: None

Label: Warners

Recorded in: N/A

Personnel:
Rod Stewart
Jim Cregan
Gary Grainger
Steve Cropper
Billy Peek
Fred Tacket
Phil Chen
Carmine Appice

Producer:
Tom Dowd

1. Do Ya Think I'm Sexy? (5:31)
2. Dirty Weekend (2:36)
3. Ain't Love a Bitch (4:39)
4. The Best Days of My Life (4:21)
5. Is That the Thanks I Get? (4:32)
6. Attractive Female Wanted (4:17)
7. Blondes (Have More Fun) (3:46)
8. Last Summer (4:05)
9. Standin' in the Shadows of Love (4:28)
10. Scarred and Scared (4:54)

Total album length: 43 minutes

Rod Stewart

Blondes have more fun

62 Cosmo's Factory

| • **Album sales:** 4,100,000 | • **Release date:** September 1970 |

If the late 1960s and early 1970s was a time of psychedelic experimentation, John and Tom Fogerty of Creedence Clearwater Revival preferred authentic rock 'n' roll, perfectly delivered as the classic pop single. *Cosmo's Factory*—named by drummer Doug Clifford after their studio's production-line knack of churning out the hits—contained more hit singles than any of their previous albums, including three Top Five singles: "Travelin' Band," "Up Around the Bend," and "Looking Out My Back Door."

The album went to Number One on both sides of the Atlantic, achieved multi-platinum status, and became Creedence Clearwater Revival's all-time best-seller both in the US (with a 69-week run on the *Billboard* charts) and worldwide.

Cosmo's Factory also sees the band attempting to look beyond their rock 'n' roll roots. Alongside trusty covers of early hits by Roy Orbison and Elvis Presley, the band take on Marvin Gaye's "I Heard It Through the Grapevine," stretching it out to an 11-minute jam.

Internal problems would later see the band implode amid acrimony and legal writs, but for a short time they led the pack. Doug Clifford and bassist Stu Cook later formed a band called Creedence Clearwater Revisited, but, after legal action by John Fogerty, were forced to change their name. The new name they chose was Cosmo's Factory.

Number One singles:
None

Grammy Awards: None

Label: US: Fantasy;
UK: Liberty

Recorded in: N/A

Personnel:
Doug "Cosmo" Clifford
Tom Fogerty
Stu Cook
John Fogerty

Producer:
John Fogerty

1. Ramble Tamble (7:10)
2. Before You Accuse Me (3:27)
3. Travelin' Band (2:07)
4. Ooby Dooby (2:07)
5. Lookin' Out My Back Door (2:35)
6. Run Through the Jungle (3:10)
7. Up Around the Bend (2:42)
8. My Baby Left Me (2:19)
9. Who'll Stop the Rain (2:29)
10. I Heard It Through the Grapevine (11:07)
11. Long as I Can See the Light (3:33)

Total album length: 42 minutes

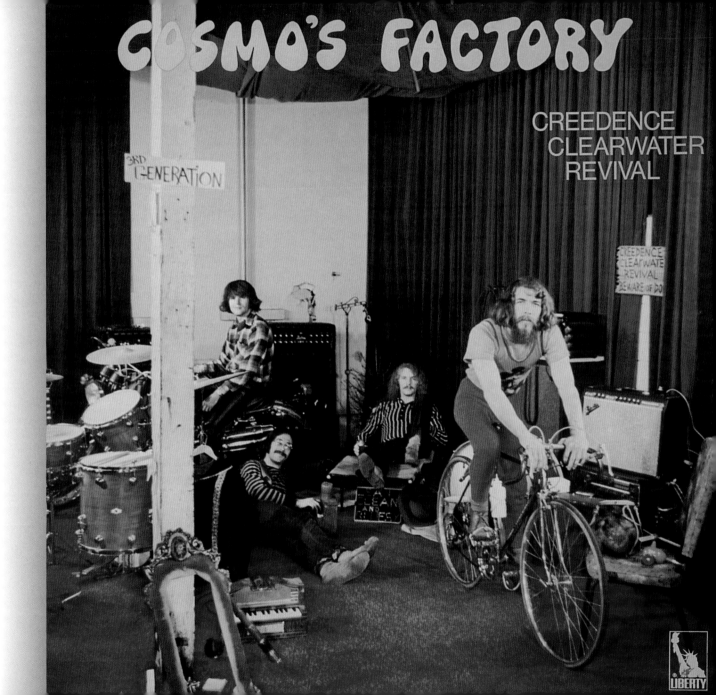

61 Fly Like an Eagle

| • **Album sales:** 4,100,000 | • **Release date:** May 1976 |

The Steve Miller who re-emerged in the spring of 1976 after almost three years without a new record was rejuvenated and clearly focused: *Fly Like an Eagle* was his most commercially accessible music yet.

Despite achieving past successes with the likes of *The Joker*, the period leading up to the making of *Fly Like an Eagle* had been so troubling personally and professionally for Miller that he took off to a remote part of Oregon and set up a farm. When he finally brought his band together to record again, they cut 22 tracks in just two weeks.

Fly Like an Eagle was released in May 1976, featuring Lonnie Turner on bass and Gary Mallaber on drums. What these sessions produced was less of the blues feel of the past and a switch to a more mainstream, melodic pop-rock sound. The change is illustrated by "Rock'n Me," which, with a nod to Free's "All Right Now," was originally just a "throwaway" song written for a UK festival appearance in July 1975, but became Miller's second Hot 100 Number One.

Fly Like an Eagle spawned two single smashes: the title track and "Take the Money and Run," while the album itself hit Number Three in the US and Number 11 in the UK in May 1976. It spent 97 weeks on the charts.

Number One singles:
US: "Rock'n Me"

Grammy Awards: None

Label: US: Capitol;
UK: Mercury

Recorded in:
San Francisco, USA

Personnel:
Steve Miller
Lonnie Turner
Gary Mallaber

Producer:
Steve Miller

1. Space Intro (1:14)
2. Fly Like an Eagle (4:55)
3. Wild Mountain Honey (4:51)
4. Serenade (3:13)
5. Dance, Dance, Dance (2:17)
6. Mercury Blues (3:30)
7. Take the Money and Run (3:14)
8. Rock'n Me (3:22)
9. You Send Me (2:42)
10. Blue Odyssey (0:53)
11. Sweet Maree (4:04)
12. The Window (4:19)

Total album length: 38 minutes

STEVE MILLER BAND
FLY LIKE AN EAGLE

60 Candy-O

| • Album sales: 4,100,000 | • Release date: October 1979 |

With UK producer Roy Thomas Baker once again behind the decks, Ric Ocasek and his Cars colleagues produced a follow-up to their hugely successful eponymous debut with more of the same quirky, offbeat songs that had caused such a stir first time round.

Tracks such as "Let's Go," the album's first single, which reached Number 14 on the US Hot 100, and the more laidback "It's All I Can Do," give ample evidence of the band's range, but the core to their material remains their electronic dabbling combined with out-and-out modern, guitar-led pop-rock.

When the Boston-hailing band released *Candy-O*—the "O" stands for "obnoxious,"

according to frontman Ocasek—new wave had already usurped punk in the UK, where in the early stages of their career the band had found a natural home. In America, though, The Cars were seen as quite cutting-edge, even "difficult." Still, this did not prevent the band from scoring their first Top Three album in the US—of all their releases, their best chart performance. In the UK, the album hit the Number 30 spot.

The album cover, which prompted allegations of sexism at the time, is by legendary pin-up artist Alberto Vargas. The model, who briefly dated drummer David Robinson, is the appropriately named Candy Moore.

Number One singles:	Personnel:
None	Ric Ocasek
	Elliot Easton
Grammy Awards: None	Greg Hawkes
	Benjamin Orr
Label: US & UK: Elektra	David Robinson
Recorded in: Los Angeles, USA	**Producer:**
	Roy Thomas Baker

1. Let's Go (3:33)
2. Since I Held You (3:16)
3. It's All I Can Do (3:44)
4. Double Life (4:14)
5. Shoo Be Doo (1:36)
6. Candy-O (2:36)
7. Night Spots (3:15)
8. You Can't Hold on Too Long (2:46)
9. Lust for Kicks (3:52)
10. Got a Lot on My Head (2:59)
11. Dangerous Type (4:28)

Total album length: 38 minutes

THE **CARS**
CANDY - O

Sleeve artwork by David Robinson and Alberto Vargas

59 | 4 Way Street

| • **Album sales:** 4,150,000 | • **Release date:** April 1971 |

Crosby, Stills, Nash & Young had split nearly a year before this live set was released, and listening to the record, fans of the band would have only mourned their demise all the more. Versions of Crosby, Stills, Nash & Young classics such as "Teach Your Children" and "Long Time Gone," together with the extended version of "Southern Man," Young's swipe at the bigotry of America's Deep South, are all as sharp as ever, if occasionally self-indulgent on the part of individual band members.

Recorded at Filmore East, in New York, the Chicago Auditorium, and The Forum, Los Angeles, the album is divided between an acoustic set, which ends with a medley of classic Young tracks, and an electric one. It includes a searing version of "Ohio," Young's protest song about four students at Kent State University who were shot dead by National Guard members three years earlier during an anti-Vietnam War demonstration.

Coming so soon after the band's split—and subsequently tapping into a demand for more CSN&Y material—the album sold particularly well, topping the US Hot 100 and achieving a Number Five placing in the UK.

Number One singles:	**Personnel:**
None	David Crosby
	Stephen Stills
Grammy Awards: None	Graham Nash
	Neil Young
Label: US & UK: Atlantic	
	Producers:
Recorded in: New York,	Crosby, Stills, Nash &
Chicago, & Los Angeles,	Young
USA	

1. Suite: Judy Blue Eyes (0:34)
2. On the Way Home (3:47)
3. Teach Your Children (3:02)
4. Triad (6:55)
5. The Lee Shore (4:28)
6. Chicago (3:10)
7. Right Between the Eyes (3:36)
8. Cowgirl in the Sand (3:58)
9. Don't Let it Bring You Down (3:30)
10. 49 Bye-Byes/America's Children (6:35)
11. Love the One You're With (3:25)
12. Pre-Road Downs (3:04)
13. Long Time Gone (5:58)
14. Southern Man (13:45)
15. Ohio (3:34)
16. Carry On (14:19)
17. Find the Cost of Freedom (2:21)

Total album length: 1 hour 27 minutes

CROSBY, STILLS, NASH & YOUNG

4 WAY STREET

58 Behind Closed Doors

| • **Album sales:** 4,150,000 | • **Release date:** February 1973 |

Charlie Rich finally hit the bigtime in 1973 with the lush countrypolitan smash *Behind Closed Doors*. Some critics panned his work as bland and safe, and certainly the album does little credit to Rich's versatility as a singer and talented pianist. Indeed, legendary Elvis producer Sam Phillips, who had signed Rich to Sun Records in 1957, was once moved to make the claim that the artist had the talent to be the only serious rival to Presley.

Again working with heavyweight producer Billy Sherrill, *Behind Closed Doors* was string-heavy, slick, and unashamed in its commercial ambitions. Rich needed a hit, and this delivered in spades. The title track made Number One on the country charts and crossed into the mainstream with a Top 20 place on the pop charts. Country purists may have objected, but the album made Rich a superstar, with a slew of awards including Country Music Association (CMA) honors for album, single, male vocalist of the year, and entertainer of the year. The Academy of Country Music (ACM) pitched in with a similar set of awards, and Rich received a Grammy for the title track.

Rich had made better music, but never more popular, and he set the template for early 1970s commercial country. His "closed doors" opened the door for adult, romantic confessional songwriting—even if Grand Ole Opry regulars in Nashville did not like it.

Number One singles:
None

Grammy Awards: Best Country Performance

Label: Epic

Recorded in:
Nashville, USA

Personnel:
Charlie Rich
The Nashville Edition
The Jordanaires

Producer:
Billy Sherrill

1. If You Wouldn't Be My Lady (2:53)
2. You Never Really Wanted Me (2:27)
3. A Sunday Kind of Woman (3:09)
4. Peace on You (3:59)
5. The Most Beautiful Girl (2:43)
6. I Take it on Home (2:52)
7. 'Til I Can't Take It Anymore (2:30)
8. We Love Each Other (3:08)
9. I'm Not Going Hungry Anymore (2:12)
10. Nothing in the World (To Do With Me) (2:41)
11. Behind Closed Doors (2:56)

Total album length: 32 minutes

Charlie Rich

STEREO
Epic
EPC 65716

CHARLIE RICH

BEHIND CLOSED DOORS

If You Wouldn't Be My Lady
You Never Really Wanted Me
A Sunday Kind Of Woman
Peace On You
The Most Beautiful Girl
I Take It On Home
'Til I Can't Take It Anymore
We Love Each Other
I'm Not Going Hungry Anymore
Nothing In The World (To Do With Me)
Behind Closed Doors

57 Rocks

| • **Album sales:** 4,150,000 | • **Release date:** June 1976 |

A Top Three album for Aerosmith in the US— it went platinum almost immediately on release—the aptly named *Rocks* is probably the band's truest, if not best, work. No compromising for radio airplay is to be found here: Guitarist Joe Perry grinds out riff after riff, the rhythm section of Tom Hamilton and Joey Kramer pound away, while frontman Tyler sings of sex, drugs, and rock 'n' roll. True, most of what one hears has been done before: "Nobody's Fault"—one of two Brad Whitford-Steve Tyler songs on the album (the other being "Last Child")—could easily have been recorded by Led Zeppelin, while The Rolling Stones could have performed "Combination" and no one would have been any the wiser.

But the twist that Aerosmith put on this kind of song is pretty unique. The album has a carnival atmosphere and there is no reverence for anything other than having a rocking good time. It was recorded at the Wherehouse in Waltham, Massachusetts, and at Record Plant Studios in New York.

Despite its US success, the album did not chart in the UK and contained no Top Ten hit for the band, although the singles "Back in the Saddle" (featuring Joe Perry playing a six-string bass) and "Last Child" were both firm radio favorites. In May 1979, readers of *Creem* magazine voted Aerosmith their Number One band and *Rocks* their favorite album.

Number One singles:
None

Grammy Awards: None

Label: US: Columbia;
UK: CBS

Recorded in: New York &
Massachusetts, USA

Personnel:
Steve Tyler
Joe Perry
Tom Hamilton
Brad Whitford
Joey Kramer
Paul Prestopino

Producers:
Jack Douglas
Aerosmith

1. **Back in the Saddle** (4:40)
2. **Last Child** (3:26)
3. **Rats in the Cellar** (4:06)
4. **Combination** (3:40)
5. **Sick as a Dog** (4:11)
6. **Nobody's Fault** (4:25)
7. **Get the Lead Out** (3:41)
8. **Lick and a Promise** (3:05)
9. **Home Tonight** (3:17)

Total album length: 34 minutes

Aerosmith

"ROCKS"

56 News of the World

| • **Album sales:** 4,150,000 | • **Release date:** November 1977 |

1977, the year that punk rock exploded in the UK, saw Queen produce its third blockbusting album in a row. The band's two previous "companion" albums, *A Night at the Opera* and *A Day at the Races*, had confirmed the four-piece as one of the best "pomp" rock acts around, but *News of the World*, which reached Number Four in the UK and Number Three in the US, took Queen to the next level, powering them to become one of the world's premier stadium acts. And what better to play in a stadium than an anthem? The album possessed two such epics in the form of "We Will Rock You" and "We Are the Champions," both of which featured on one single released in the UK and US, hitting Numbers Two and Four respectively in these countries' charts. This gave Elektra records their first two-million-selling single, while the album spent 37 weeks on the charts.

News of the World, despite being the band's quickest album to record, is no two-track wonder. It also contains brooding numbers such as "Spread Your Wings" and the jazz-like "My Melancholy Blues," together with full-speed rock tracks like "Sheer Heart Attack," regarded by many as the band's riposte to the burgeoning punk movement, which saw in Queen everything that was overblown in rock.

The album cover is by the science fiction artist Frank Kelly Freas.

Number One singles:
None

Grammy Awards: None

Label: US: Elektra;
UK: EMI

Recorded: Various
locations, UK

Personnel:
Freddie Mercury
Brian May
John Deacon
Roger Taylor

Producers:
Queen
Mike Stone

1. We Will Rock You (2:02)
2. We Are the Champions (3:01)
3. Sheer Heart Attack (3:27)
4. All Dead, All Dead (3:11)
5. Spread Your Wings (4:35)
6. Fight From the Inside (3:03)
7. Get Down, Make Love (3:51)
8. Sleep on the Sidewalk (3:08)
9. Who Needs You (3:06)
10. It's Late (6:26)
11. My Melancholy Blues (3:30)

Total album length: 39 minutes

Queen

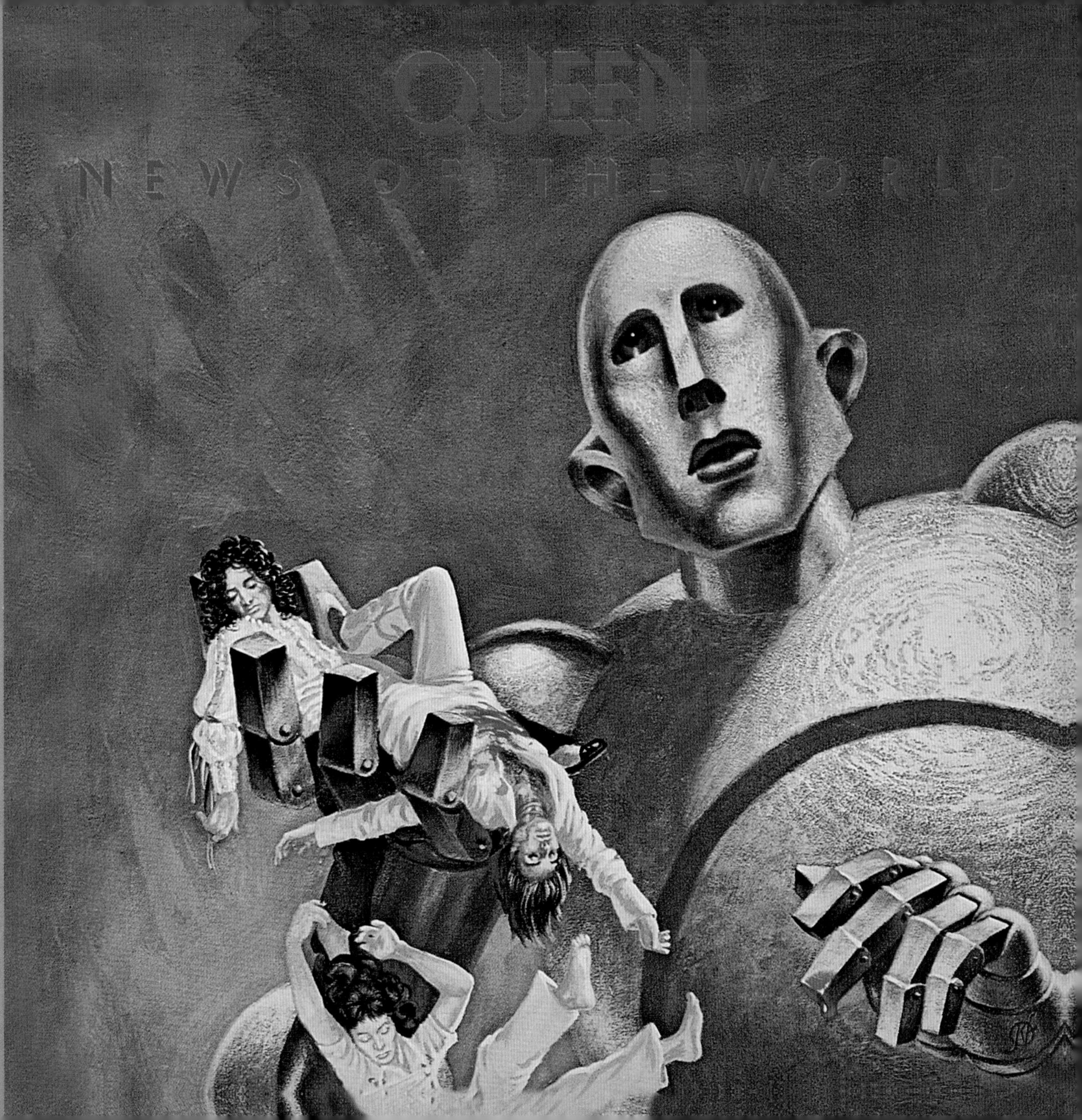

Sleeve artwork by Frank Kelly Freas

55 One of These Nights

| • **Album sales:** 4,350,000 | • **Release date:** June 1975 |

With its pin-sharp production sound and slickly crafted songs, the Eagles' fourth album became the band's first US Number One album and, thanks to the title track, provided their second US Number One single.

The Eagles' wonderful harmonies are once again in evidence, particularly on the title song, while their storytelling talents are given the full treatment on the achingly bittersweet "Lyin' Eyes"—a Number Two single in the US and a Number 23 in the UK, as well as a Grammy winner—and "After the Thrill Is Gone." Meanwhile, "Take It to the Limit" reached Number Four on the singles' chart in the US and Number 12 in the UK.

"Too Many Hands" and "Visions" are a couple of rousing rockers, while "Hollywood Waltz" is a classic Eagles' ballad. Fans of the British TV series *The Hitch-Hiker's Guide to the Galaxy* will meanwhile recognize the album's one instrumental, "Journey of the Sorceror," as the source for the program's musical theme.

The album also reached Number Eight on the UK album chart. It was, however, to mark a turning point for the band: At the year's end, country guitarist, banjo-player, and multi-instrumentalist Bernie Leadon left the band and was replaced by Joe Walsh.

Number One singles: US: "One of These Nights"

Grammy Awards: Best Pop Vocal Performance by a Duo, Group, or Chorus

Label: US & UK: Asylum

Recorded in: Miami & Los Angeles, USA

Personnel:
Don Henley
Glenn Frey
Bernie Leadon
Randy Meisner
Don Felder

Producer:
Bill Szymczyk

1. **One of These Nights** (4:51)
2. **Too Many Hands** (4:40)
3. **Hollywood Waltz** (4:01)
4. **Journey of the Sorcerer** (6:38)
5. **Lyin' Eyes** (6:21)
6. **Take It to the Limit** (4:46)
7. **Visions** (3:58)
8. **After the Thrill Is Gone** (3:56)
9. **I Wish You Peace** (3:45)

Total album length: 43 minutes

Eagles

54 A Star Is Born

| • **Album sales:** 4,350,000 | • **Release date:** November 1976 |

Barbra Streisand made a rare attempt at songwriting for *A Star Is Born* and what emerged was an Oscar-winning Number One. "Evergreen," the love theme from Streisand's tenth movie, was born out of a period of frustration in which she felt inadequate at not being able to write her own songs like some other singers. The ballad, cowritten by seasoned tunesmith and the movie's music supervisor Paul Williams, turned out to be the chief selling point of the soundtrack. It topped the Hot 100 for three weeks in March 1977, taking three Grammy Awards and the Best Song category at the Academy Awards.

Streisand added a second rare cowrite to the soundtrack, "Lost Inside of You," which she performed with costar Kris Kristofferson, while other song contributors to the album included Kenny Loggins, Rupert Holmes, and *The Way We Were* lyricists Alan and Marilyn Bergman.

A Star Is Born became Streisand's third album to reach Number One in the US, staying there for six weeks, her longest-ever chart-topping run.

Number One singles:
None

Grammy Awards: Song of the Year: "Love Theme From A Star Is Born (Evergreen)"; Best Pop Vocal Performance, Female: "Love Theme From A Star Is Born (Evergreen)"

Label: Columbia

Recorded in: Los Angeles and San Francisco, USA

Personnel:
Barbra Streisand
Kris Kristofferson

Bobby Shew
Charles Owens
Donnie Fritts
Clydie King
Stephen Bruton
Sammy Creason
Vanetta Fields
Dean Hagen
Booker T. Jones
Jerry McGee
Art Munson
The Oreos
Terry Paul
Jack Redmond
The Speedway
Mike Utley

Producers:
Barbra Streisand
Phil Ramone

1. **Watch Closely Now** (3:50)
2. **Queen Bee** (3:56)
3. **Everything** (3:50)
4. **Lost Inside of You** (2:54)
5. **Hellacious Acres** (2:58)
6. **Love Theme From A Star Is Born (Evergreen)** (3:04)
7. **The Woman in the Moon** (4:49)
8. **I Believe in Love** (3:13)
9. **Crippled Crow** (7:43)
10. **Reprise: Love Theme From A Star Is Born (Evergreen)** (1:47)

Total album length: 41 minutes

53 Breakfast in America

| • **Album sales:** 4,350,000 | • **Release date:** March 1979 |

Supertramp's fourth album, *Breakfast in America*, did what earlier efforts had singularly—or even collectively—failed to do: it broke the English band in the United States. *Breakfast in America* proved to be a huge hit both in the US and the UK; a Number One album on the US Hot 100 and a Number Three position in the UK. The album spawned four hit singles, ensuring that for a few months Supertramp were one of the most played acts on radio in both the US and the UK.

At a time when punk rock had already evolved into "new wave," pretty much on both sides of the Atlantic, Supertramp were to be found plowing the same creative furrow they had been since their formation; namely, producing rather overblown songs whose catchiness belied their musical complexity. Infectious, melodic pop songs such as "The Logical Song," "Goodbye Stranger," and "Take the Long Way Home" had mass appeal, something the band had been unable to capture with its earlier works. All three singles made it into the US Top 20; "The Logical Song" reached Number Six.

The appropriately named album, which was recorded in Los Angeles' Village Recorder studio, also prompted the band to relocate to California.

Number One singles:
None

Grammy Awards: None

Label: US & UK: A&M

Recorded in:
Los Angeles, USA

Personnel:
Rick Davies
Roger Hodgson
John A. Helliwell
Dougie Thomson
Bob C. Benberg

Producers:
Supertramp
Peter Henderson

1. Gone Hollywood (5:18)
2. The Logical Song (4:11)
3. Goodbye Stranger (5:50)
4. Breakfast in America (2:39)
5. Oh Darling (3:58)
6. Take the Long Way Home (5:08)
7. Lord Is It Mine (4:09)
8. Just Another Nervous Wreck (4:25)
9. Casual Conversations (2:58)
10. Child of Vision (7:28)

Total album length: 46 minutes

Supertramp

SUPERTRAMP
Breakfast
IN AMERICA

Sleeve artwork by Mick Haggerty and Mike Doud

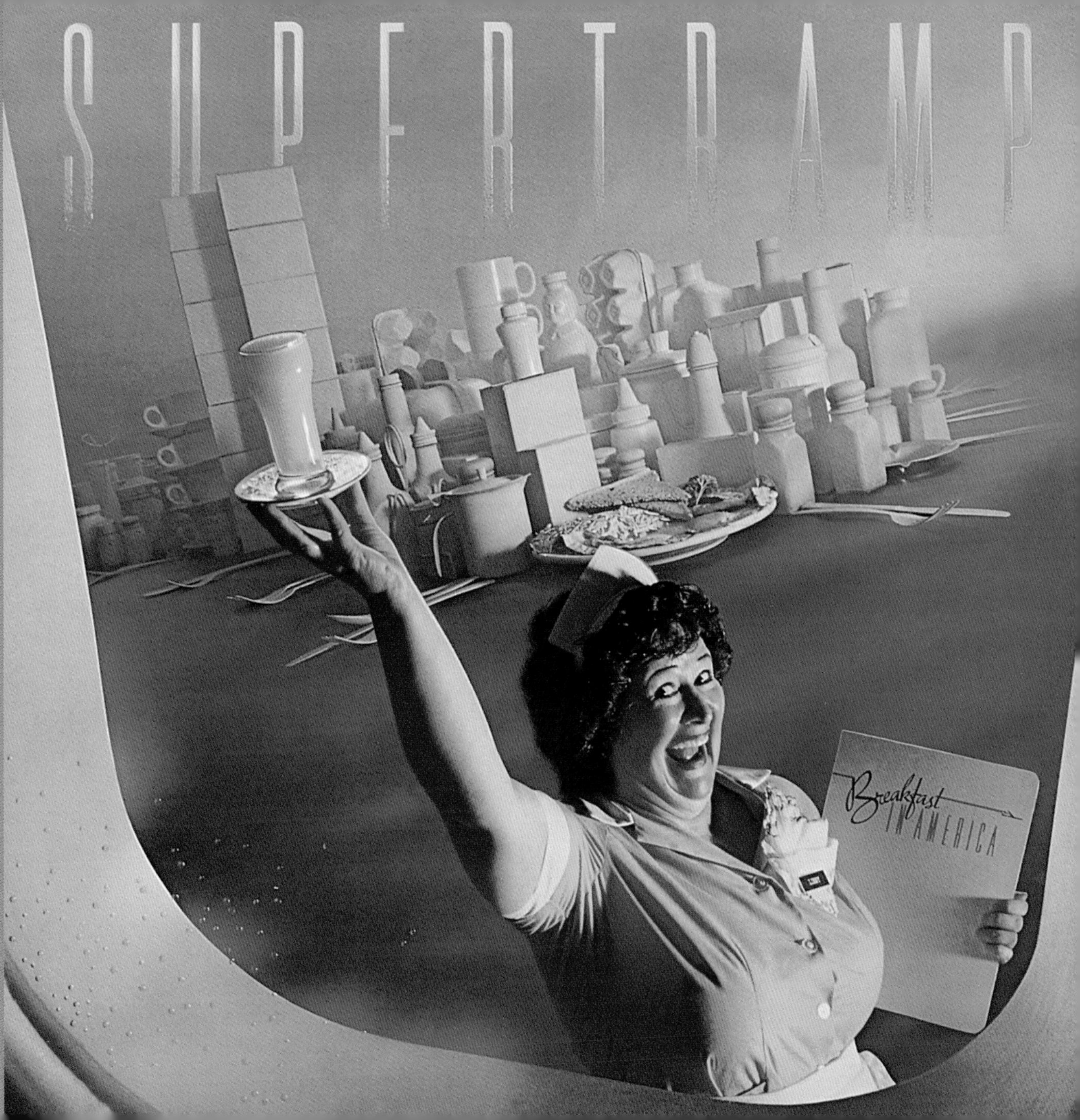

52 The Song Remains the Same

| • **Album sales:** 4,350,000 | • **Release date:** October 1976 |

Billed not as a "live" album, but as an original movie soundtrack, *The Song Remains the Same* takes its place within the Led Zeppelin canon as a multi-sales award winner, a US Number Two, and a UK chart topper. It spent 15 weeks in the UK charts and 12 weeks in the US charts.

Yet, critically and artistically, the album was the band's low point to date. Recorded at the thin end of a 1973 tour, live at Madison Square Garden, and mixed at Electric Ladyland Studios in New York, the album failed to impress. Even a banker such as "Stairway to Heaven" is marred by Robert Plant's hippieisms, while the John Bonham "drumathon" "Moby Dick" provides a persuasive argument for the economy of then-burgeoning punk rock.

A run of superb albums had placed the band as untouchable superstars and, following the career high of *Physical Graffiti*, the release of an original soundtrack to an in-concert movie seemed to make commercial sense. The movie, which was described by their manager Peter Grant as "the most expensive home movie ever made," performed respectably at the box office, despite a series of suspect fantasy sequences. Nonetheless, Zeppelin's soundtrack fails to capture the spirit of a band considered at the time to be the world's top live draw.

Number One singles:
None

Grammy Awards: None

Label: US & UK: Swan Song

Recorded in: New York, USA

Personnel:
Robert Plant
John Paul Jones
John Bonham
Jimmy Page

Producers:
Jimmy Page
Peter Grant

1. **Rock and Roll** (4:03)
2. **Celebration Day** (3:49)
3. **The Song Remains the Same** (5:53)
4. **Rain Song** (8:25)
5 **Dazed and Confused** (26:52)
6. **No Quarter** (12:30)
7. **Stairway to Heaven** (10:57)
8. **Moby Dick** (12:46)
9. **Whole Lotta Love** (14:25)

Total album length: 1 hour 39 minutes

Led Zeppelin

THE SOUNDTRACK FROM THE FILM

LED·ZEPPELIN

THE SONG REMAINS THE SAME

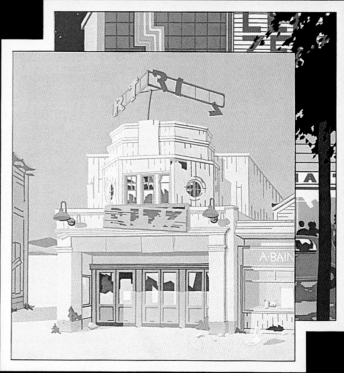

Sleeve artwork by Hipgnosis and George Hardie

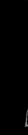

51 Paranoid

• **Album sales:** 4,500,000 | • **Release date:** September 1970

Full of dark, brooding—almost dirgelike—heavy metal, *Paranoid* was Black Sabbath's second album and the record that not only confirmed their commercial status in their UK homeland—it topped the UK charts within weeks of its release—but also broke the band in the US, reaching Number 12, bettering their debut's best chart achievement by 11 places.

The material is undoubtedly relentless and gloomy, with songs about death, pestilence, war, disease, and the hallucinations that result from too much drinking and imbibing too many illegal substances. Tracks such as "War Pigs," "Paranoid," and "Hand of Doom" all conveyed dark cynicism wrapped in a thundering, driving beat, thanks to Geezer Butler's unique bass style and Bill Ward's no-nonsense drumming. Ozzy Osbourne's distinctive vocals and Tony Iommi's grinding guitar riffs complement the rhythm section admirably. Sabbath's distinctive sound also owes something to gruesome accident: Iommi cut off the tip of his finger before the release of the band's debut, forcing him to tune his guitar down half a step so that it was less painful to play.

The album's title track was an immediate single success in the UK, reaching Number Four. The band called themselves Black Sabbath after a 1935 Boris Karloff movie.

Number One singles: None

Grammy Awards: None

Label: US: Warner; UK: Vertigo

Recorded in: London, UK

Personnel:
Tony Iommi
Ozzy Osbourne
Geezer Butler
Bill Ward

Producer:
Rodger Bain

1. **War Pigs** (7:55)
2. **Paranoid** (2:50)
3. **Planet Caravan** (4:30)
4. **Iron Man** (6:00)
5. **Electric Funeral** (4:50)
6. **Hand of Doom** (7:10)
7. **Rat Salad** (2:30)
8. **Fairies Wear Boots** (6:15)

Total album length: 40 minutes

Black Sabbath

50 Let It Be

| • **Album sales:** 4,550,000 | • **Release date:** May 1970 |

Let It Be set out with the worthy intention of returning The Beatles to their raw, early recording days, but ended up creating yet more internal arguments among a band falling apart.

Despite various attempts at compiling an album from the sessions, the whole project's release was shelved and only revisited once *Abbey Road* had been recorded and the group had effectively broken up.

In a move that angered Paul McCartney, Phil Spector was given the tricky task of sifting through the recordings; an album was finally issued in May 1970. With John Lennon's few contributions including two revived songs, a re-recording of a 1963 cut "One After 909" and "Across the Universe," originally part of a 1968 charity album, the tracklisting is dominated by McCartney. Three of his tracks were US Number One singles—the old-fashioned rock 'n' roller "Get Back," one of several tracks featuring Billy Preston on keyboards, the hymnlike "Let It Be," and "The Long and Winding Road," in which Spector overdubbed orchestration and a female choir to the fury of its author.

The album predictably topped the UK album charts and was a four-week chart topper in the US, where it replaced McCartney's own solo debut (simply titled *McCartney*) at Number One. A new version of *Let It Be*, stripped of Phil Spector's influence, was released in 2003.

Number One singles:
US & UK: "Get Back";
US: "Let It Be"; "The Long and Winding Road"

Grammy Awards: None

Label: US & UK: Apple

Recorded in: London, UK

Personnel:
John Lennon
Paul McCartney
George Harrison
Ringo Starr
Billy Preston

Producer:
Phil Spector

1. Two of Us (3:37)
2. Dig a Pony (3:54)
3. Across the Universe (3:49)
4. I Me Mine (2:26)
5. Dig It (0:50)
6. Let It Be (4:03)
7. Maggie Mae (0:41)
8. I've Got a Feeling (3:38)
9. One After 909 (2:55)
10. The Long and Winding Road (3:38)
11. For You Blue (2:33)
12. Get Back (3:07)

Total album length: 35 minutes

LET IT BE

Animals

| • Album sales: 4,550,000 | • Release date: February 1977 |

Fans of Pink Floyd had become well accustomed to the band's conceptual approach to their music by the time *Animals* surfaced in the early part of 1977, but few can have expected the quirky album that followed the electronic grandeur that was *Wish You Were Here*. Nevertheless, despite being positively "lo-fi" compared with earlier efforts, *Animals* continues the policy of thematic creativity to great effect.

An album seemingly about man's best friend and two of the more familiar farmyard creatures, as with all things Floyd there is more to this than meets the eye—and ear. Using the animal kingdom as a metaphor for humanity's weaknesses, the band—and songwriter Roger

Waters in particular—look at death, decay, avarice, sex, power, jealousy, and more, much more. On "Pigs (Three Different Ones)" there is even a dig at Mary Whitehouse, the British personality whose crusading calls throughout the 1970s for a return to the wholesome "values" of the past landed her with the title of unofficial guardian of the nation's morals.

As well as themes, *Animals* contained other Pink Floyd trademarks such as numerous intricate guitar solos courtesy of Dave Gilmour, but the album appears to have struck less of a chord with US audiences than its immediate predecessors, peaking at Number Three on the Hot 100, while it managed Number Two in the UK. *Animals* spent 28 weeks on the charts and received its triple platinum certification in 1989.

Number One singles:
None

Grammy Awards: None

Label: US: Columbia;
UK: Harvest

Recorded in: London, UK

Personnel:
Dave Gilmour
Roger Waters
Rick Wright
Nick Mason

Producer:
Pink Floyd

1. **Pigs on the Wing (Part One)** (1:25)
2. **Dogs** (17:04)
3. **Pigs (Three Different Ones)** (11:21)
4. **Sheep** (10:23)
5. **Pigs on the Wing (Part Two)** (1:24)

Total album length: 41 minutes

Pink Floyd

Harvest

| • **Album sales:** 4,650,000 | • **Release date:** March 1972 |

Coming two years after the demise of Crosby, Stills, Nash & Young, *Harvest*, which topped both the US and UK charts on its release, remains probably Neil Young's most popular work.

Many of the songs are riven with melancholy, whether they cover the quest for a relationship ("A Man Needs a Maid") or bear witness to a friend's demise through drug addiction ("The Needle and the Damage Done"). There is also something almost obscenely simple about the title track, with its tale of unrequited—and unwanted—love set against a see-sawing country rhythm and plaintive pedal steel guitar.

Having slipped a disc, Young recorded much of *Harvest* wearing a back brace. "That's a lot of the reason it's such a mellow album," he later said. "I couldn't physically play an electric guitar."

Songs such as "Old Man" were recorded in Nashville, but "A Man Needs a Maid" was completed with the accompaniment of the London Symphony Orchestra at, perhaps surprisingly, Barking Assembly Hall in London's East End.

Although "Heart of Gold" topped the charts in the US and reached Number Ten in the UK, the song's popularity left Young uncomfortable: "It put me in the middle of the road. Traveling there soon became a bore so I headed for the ditch." The song remains his only Top Ten hit.

Number One singles:
US: "Heart of Gold"

Grammy Awards: None

Label: US & UK: Reprise

Recorded in: Nashville, Tennessee, USA; Barking Assembly Hall, London, UK, & various other locations

Personnel:
Neil Young
Ben Keith
Tim Drummond
Jack Nitzsche
Kenny Buttrey
James Taylor

Producers:
Neil Young
Elliot Mazer
Jack Nitzsche
Henry Lewy

1. Out on the Weekend (4:34)
2. Harvest (3:11)
3. A Man Needs a Maid (4:05)
4. Heart of Gold (3:07)
5. Are You Ready For the Country? (3:23)
6. Old Man (3:24)
7. There's a World (2:59)
8. Alabama (4:02)
9. The Needle and the Damage Done (2:03)
10. Words (Between the Lines of Age) (6:40)

Total album length: 37 minutes

47 The Gambler

| • **Album sales:** 5,050,000 | • **Release date:** November 1978 |

Kenny Rogers hit the jackpot with *The Gambler*, securing a new signature tune, one of his biggest-ever crossover albums, and even the start of an acting career.

By the time of its release in November 1978, Rogers was already established as a country music veteran, but these recordings pushed him in front of a whole new audience and placed him among America's Top 20 pop artists for the first time. The album's title track went on to top the *Billboard* country chart at the end of 1978, reach the pop Top 20, win a Grammy, and give birth to a small screen movie of the same name starring Rogers himself.

"She Believes in Me," another country Number One, was an even bigger crossover favorite as it topped America's adult contemporary chart and equaled his then Hot 100 peak of Number Five. The album lifted Rogers to his highest position at that point of Number 12 on the *Billboard* 200 album chart in March 1979.

Number One singles:
None

Grammy Awards: Best Country Vocal Performance, Male: "The Gambler"

Label: United Artists

Recorded in: Nashville, USA

Personnel:
Kenny Rogers
Tommy Allsup
Pete Drake
Tony Joe White
Eddie Anderson
Mickey Newbury
The Jordanaires
Bill Medley
Byron Bach
George Minkley III
Thoms Cain
Jimmy Capps
Jerry Carrigan
Marvin Chantry
Bobby Daniels
Randy Dorman
Eay Edenton
Steve Glassmeyer
Gene Golden
Lennie Haight
Ricky Harper
Sheldon Kurland
Byron Metcalf
Various other personnel

Producer:
Larry Butler

1. The Gambler (3:34)
2. I Wish That I Could Hurt That Way Again (2:58)
3. The King of Oak Street (5:05)
4. Making Music For Money (3:18)
5. The Hooddoin' of Miss Fannie Deberry (4:45)
6. She Believes in Me (4:15)
7. Tennessee Bottle (4:02)
8. Sleep Tight, Goodnight Man (2:55)
9. A Little More Like Me (The Crucifixion) (2:50)
10. San Francisco Mabel Joy (3:41)
11. Morgana Jones (3:07)

Total album length: 36 minutes

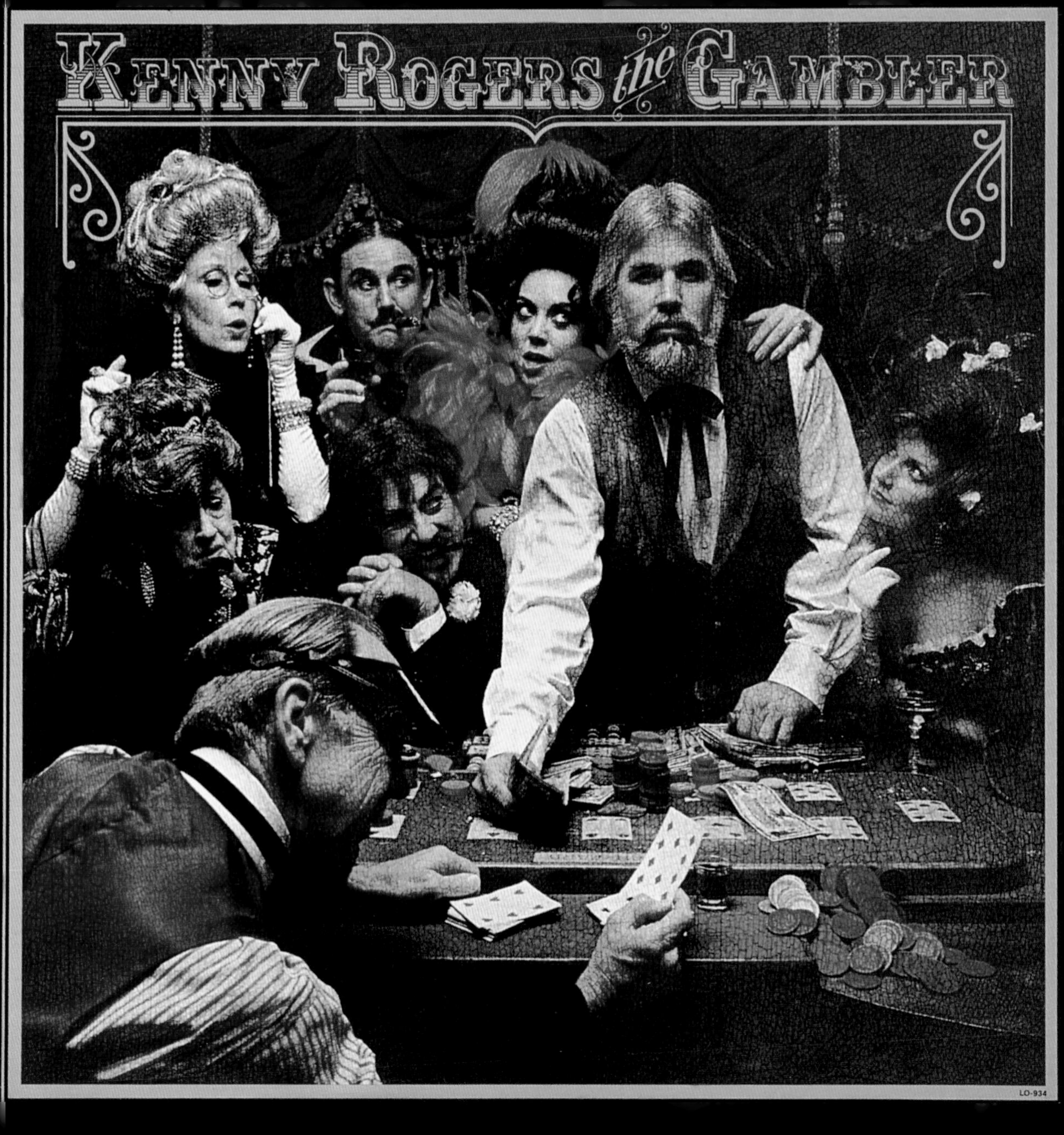
KENNY ROGERS the GAMBLER
LO-934

46 Head Games

| • **Album sales:** 5,050,000 | • **Release date:** September 1979 |

By the time *Head Games* hit the shelves of record stores around the world, Foreigner had overcome their initial trepidation at having seen their career take off so remarkably and were now firmly established as one of the biggest arena rock acts in America.

Having suffered at the hands of the critics for entertaining a sound that was too polished, the band now made an effort to sound rougher round the edges. The album's earthy opener, "Dirty White Boy," certainly fits the bill, although Mick Jones had to deny accusations that the song had racist overtones.

While "Women" is another gritty song, elsewhere the album reverts to type, with a typical grandiose rocker, "Love on the Telephone," the good-feeling "The Modern Day," and the title track, which exudes everything "big-sounding" that Foreigner fans had come to expect.

The record sees the Foreigner debut of bassist Rick Wills (ex-Roxy Music and Small Faces), following the departure of Ed Gagliardi.

"Dirty White Boy" and "Head Games" were US Top 20 singles. The album peaked at Number Five on the US album charts, spending 41 weeks in the chart, but failed to make the Top 40 in the UK.

Number One singles:
None

Grammy Awards: None

Label: US & UK: Atlantic

Recorded in: New York, USA

Personnel:
Lou Gramm
Mick Jones
Ian McDonald
Al Greenwood
Rick Wills
Dennis Elliott

Producers:
Roy Thomas Baker
Mick Jones
Ian McDonald

1. Dirty White Boy (3:38)
2. Love on the Telephone (3:17)
3. Women (3:24)
4. I'll Get Even With You (3:39)
5. Seventeen (4:35)
6. Head Games (3:37)
7. The Modern Day (3:26)
8. Blinded By Science (4:55)
9. Do What You Like (3:58)
10. Rev on the Red Line (3:41)

Total album length: 42 minutes

FOREIGNER

head games

45 | Foreigner

• **Album sales:** 5,100,000 | • **Release date:** March 1977

Essentially the brainchild of ex-Spooky Tooth guitarist Mick Jones, the Anglo-US Foreigner very nearly didn't get the record deal that enabled them to thrust themselves onto the world's airwaves with their debut album. Record companies that they approached apparently didn't hear a hit in the band's demos, despite the completed album going on to spawn such hits as "Feels Like the First Time" and "Cold as Ice."

The band would become one of the biggest rock acts of the late 1970s–early 1980s and, after Led Zeppelin, Atlantic's biggest-selling international act.

In addition to the two hit singles, the album featured slick production values and the even slicker guitar work of Mick Jones, together with the soaring voice of singer Lou Gramm. The blend of melody and pure rock 'n' roll riffs ensured the album's—and subsequently the band's—success. "Feels Like the First Time" and "Cold as Ice" went to Number Four and Six on the US singles chart respectively, while the album also went to Number Four on the US album chart, spending 113 weeks on the charts altogether. In the then-punk dominated UK, it managed a more sedate Number 24 on its release in the summer of 1978.

Number One singles:
None

Grammy Awards: None

Label: US & UK: Atlantic

Recorded in: New York, USA

Personnel:
Lou Gramm
Mick Jones
Ian McDonald
Al Greenwood
Ed Gagliardi
Dennis Elliott

Producers:
John Sinclair
Gary Lyons
Mick Jones
Ian McDonald

1. Feels Like the First Time (3:53)
2. Cold as Ice (3:23)
3. Starrider (4:03)
4. Headknocker (3:05)
5. The Damage Is Done (4:19)
6. Long, Long Way From Home (2:55)
7. Woman Oh Woman (3:53)
8. At War With the World (4:26)
9. Fool For You Anyway (4:17)
10. I Need You (5:18)

Total album length: 38 minutes

44 Silk Degrees

| • **Album sales:** 5,150,000 | • **Release date:** March 1976 |

As an R&B singer inclining more to pop and rock, the mid-1970s saw Boz Scaggs take the commercially and artistically crucial decision to quit collaborating with producer Johnny Bristol and team up with Columbia staff producer Joe Wissert, who had been working the magic for Earth, Wind & Fire.

Assembling a studio band including bassist David Hungate, drummer Jeff Porcaro, and keyboard player and arranger David Paich (who would all later form the foundation of Toto), the results captured the FM airwaves. *Silk Degrees* reached Number Two in the US and Number 20 in the UK. "Lowdown" was a Top Three single,

and "Lido Shuffle," "It's Over," and "What Can I Say" all made solid chart showings. Another standout track, the Scaggs-penned "We're All Alone," was later a Top 10 hit for Rita Coolidge.

Scaggs now inhabited a world far away from the futuristic work he had produced as a member of Steve Miller's band in the late 1960s. "Lido Shuffle" was a synthesizer and horn-powered romp, while the more considered "Lowdown" picked up a Grammy for best rhythm & blues song. With *Silk Degrees*, Scaggs finally had the right songs, the right setting, and the right suit. The album stayed on the charts for more than 100 weeks and earned platinum status, although Scaggs was never able to repeat its success.

Number One singles:
None

Grammy Awards: Best Rhythm & Blues Song: "Lowdown"

Label: US: Columbia; UK: CBS

Recorded in: Los Angeles, USA

Personnel:
Boz Scaggs
David Paich
Jeff Porcaro
Fred Tackett
Les Dudek
Louie Shelton
David Hungate

Producer:
Joe Wissert

1. What Can I Say (3:01)
2. Georgia (3:55)
3. Jump Street (5:11)
4. What Do You Want the Girl To Do? (3:52)
5. Harbor Lights (5:56)
6. Lowdown (5:16)
7. It's Over (2:50)
8. Love Me Tomorrow (3:15)
9. Lido Shuffle (3:41)
10. We're All Alone (4:12)

Total album length: 41 minutes

BOZ SCAGGS *SILK DEGREES*

Sleeve artwork by Ron Coro, Moshe Brakha, and Nancy Donald

43 Abraxas

| • **Album sales:** 5,200,000 | • **Release date:** November 1970 |

Fusing African and Latin rhythms with rock 'n' roll more successfully than probably any other recording artist of his day, Carlos Santana's second album, recorded at Wally Heider Studio in San Francisco, woke the world up to the potential of music that crossed genre and territorial boundaries.

The follow-up to *Santana*, the band's hugely successful debut, *Abraxas* is a mesmerizing record, with subtle, laid-back grooves melding effortlessly with modern rock, and all performed with a Latin twist. African rhythms are in abundance on songs such as "El Nicoya," while the Latin sound is ever-present on tracks like "Samba Pa Ti." But pure rock is never far away either, with "Hope You're Feeling Better" amply illustrating Santana's dexterity with a rock-styled guitar riff.

Abraxas also features two of Santana's best-known tracks: first a medley that blends Fleetwood Mac founder Peter Green's "Black Magic Woman" into Gabor Szabo's "Gypsy Queen"; second a cover of Tito Puente's "Oye Como Va." Both tracks were big hits in the US, reaching Number Four and Number 13 on the singles chart respectively, while the album topped the US charts and stayed there for an impressive six weeks. In the UK, the album peaked at Number Seven.

Number One singles:
None

Grammy Awards: None

Label: US: Columbia;
UK: CBS

Recorded in: San
Francisco, USA

Personnel:
Carlos Santana
Gregg Rolie
Dave Brown
Mike Shrieve
Jose Areas
Mike Carabello
Rico Reyes
Alberto Gianquinto

Producers:
Fred Catero
Santana

1. **Singing Winds, Crying Beasts** (4:51)
2. **Black Magic Woman/Gypsy Queen** (5:19)
3. **Oye Como Va** (4:19)
4. **Incident at Neshabur** (5:00)
5. **Se A Cabo** (2:52)
6. **Mother's Daughter** (4:28)
7. **Samba Pa Ti** (4:47)
8. **Hope You're Feeling Better** (4:17)
9. **El Nicoya** (1:39)

Total album length: 36 minutes

42 Aloha From Hawaii

| • **Album sales:** 5,200,000 | • **Release date:** February 1973 |

The live shows that Elvis Presley threw himself into from the end of the 1960s—after an eight-year concert absence—reached critical mass in January 1973, when he played an hour-long set in Honolulu. Not only did he perform for an auditorium audience of thousands, but also—in something of a technological breakthrough for the time—the concert was broadcast by satellite to an estimated one billion people around the world.

By the time the show took place, RCA had already received advance orders for millions of copies of the accompanying double album. When it was released a month later, *Aloha From Hawaii* became Presley's first album since 1964's *Roustabout* to top the US Hot 100, replacing Pink Floyd's *Dark Side of the Moon* before making way a week later for Led Zeppelin's *Houses of the Holy*.

The recording captures Presley performing early favorites such as "Hound Dog" and "Blue Suede Shoes" alongside more contemporary tracks like "Burning Love," "Suspicious Minds," and "Early Morning Rain."

Number one singles: None	**Personnel:** Elvis Presley J.D. Sumner & The Stamps
Grammy Awards: None	Kathy Westmoreland The Sweet Inspirations
Label: US & UK: RCA	
Recorded in: Honolulu, USA	**Producer:** Joan Deary

1. Introduction: Also Sprach Zarathustra (1:11)
2. See See Rider (2:59)
3. Burning Love (2:56)
4. Something (3:46)
5. You Gave Me a Mountain (3:16)
6. Steamroller Blues (3:09)
7. My Way (4:04)
8. Love Me (1:55)
9. Johnny B. Goode (1:43)
10. It's Over (2:08)
11. Blue Suede Shoes (1:16)
12. I'm So Lonesome I Could Cry (2:17)
13. I Can't Stop Loving You (2:28)
14. Hound Dog (1:06)
15. What Now My Love (3:12)
16. Fever (2:41)
17. Welcome To My World (2:00)
18. Suspicious Minds (4:31)
19. Introduction by Elvis (2:42)
20. I'll Remember You (2:33)
21. Long Tall Sally/Whole Lotta Shakin' Goin' On (2:05)
22. An American Trilogy (4:43)
23. A Big Hunk O' Love (2:14)
24. Can't Help Falling in Love (2:26)
25. Blue Hawaii (2:31)
26. Ku-U-I-Po (2:04)
27. No More (2:28)
28. Hawaiian Wedding Song (1:54)
29. Early Morning Rain (2:53)

Total album length:
1 hour 15 minutes

ELVIS
Aloha from Hawaii
via SATELLITE

Sleeve artwork by Jacqueline Murphy and Joseph A. Tunzi

RCA

DPS 2040 (VPSX 6089)

2 RECORD SET

41 Bad Co.

• **Album sales:** 5,250,000 | • **Release date:** June 1974

Born out of the embers of three of the UK's leading rock outfits—Free, Mott The Hoople, and King Crimson—Bad Company were snapped up by Led Zeppelin manager Peter Grant to record for his fledgling Swan Song label. The band then took advantage of a two-week break in Led Zeppelin's recording schedule at Headley Grange to record their own album there.

Bad Company's live debut came in the summer of 1974 at the UK's Newcastle City Hall, before following up with an opening slot for The Edgar Winter Group Tour in the US. With their album released at the same time, Bad Company established themselves pretty much immediately on both sides of the Atlantic.

Basic, no-nonsense bar-room rock 'n' roll the album may have been, with rather predictable lyrics about not being able to get enough love and the need to keep on "moving 'n' ramblin'," but that didn't stop *Bad Co.* topping the US Hot 100, spending 64 weeks on the charts and reaching Number Three in the UK. Thanks to its Wild West imagery, the album very much foreshadows similar fare from the likes of Bon Jovi some 20 or so years later.

"Can't Get Enough," the album's opener, is a surefire classic rock love song, as is "Bad Company." The album is not devoid of lilting ballads, however, with gospel-tinged "Don't Let Me Down" and the acoustic "Seagull" among the highlights.

Number One singles:
None

Grammy Awards:
None

Label: US: Swan Song; UK: Island

Recorded in:
Hampshire, UK

Personnel:
Paul Rogers
Mick Ralphs
Boz Burrell
Simon Kirke

Producer:
Bad Company

1. **Can't Get Enough** (4:16)
2. **Rock Steady** (3:47)
3. **Ready For Love** (5:02)
4. **Don't Let Me Down** (4:21)
5. **Bad Company** (4:50)
6. **The Way I Choose** (5:05)
7. **Movin' On** (3:24)
8. **Seagull** (4:02)

Total album length: 35 minutes

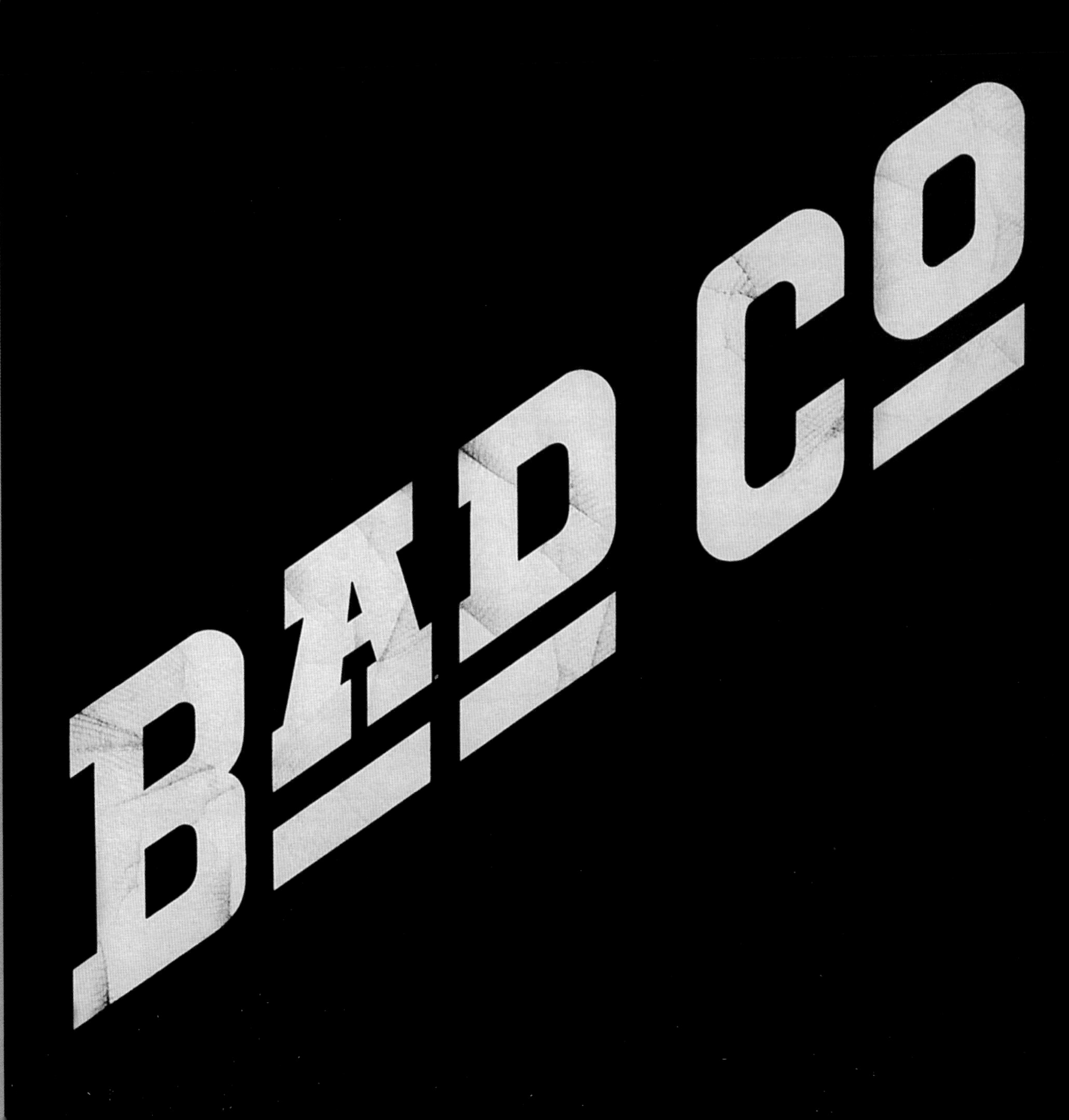
BAD CO

39 Stardust

• **Album sales:** 5,250,000 | • **Release date:** June 1978

Having popularized the concept of Outlaw country, Willie Nelson released a collection of pop standards, even though he is quite the songwriter himself, being the composer of some of Nashville's most personal songs, such as "Hello, Walls," "Crazy," and "Night Life."

Largely reassembling the winning team behind his 1975 breakthrough *Red Headed Stranger*, Nelson set out to re-create the sounds of his youth and the songs that he had grown up with on the radio, addressing the music of Hoagy Carmichael, Irving Berlin, and the Gershwins, among others. With the crucial input of producer Booker T. Jones (of MGs repute), Nelson moved from pop to folk, from jazz to country, exploring the breadth of American music. He rediscovered the wealth his roots had to offer and was unafraid to re-present that music in all its hues.

Initial label misgivings were soon replaced by acclaim as Nelson scooped Entertainer of the Year awards from both the CMA and the ACM. Repeating his 1975 success, Nelson also took a Grammy for Best Country Vocal Performance for his reading of Carmichael's "Georgia On My Mind." Now well into his forties, Nelson was enjoying the most successful period of his career. That this was achieved with a covers album makes the feat even more extraordinary.

Number One singles:
None

Grammy Awards:
Best Country Vocal
Performance, Male:
"Georgia On My Mind"

Label: Columbia

Recorded in: South
California, USA

Personnel:
Willie Nelson
Jody Payne
Bee Spears
Rex Ludwig
Bobbie Nelson
Mickey Raphael
Paul English
Chris Ethridge

Producer:
Booker T. Jones

1. Stardust (3:52)
2. Georgia On My Mind (4:20)
3. Blue Skies (3:34)
4. All of Me (3:54)
5. Unchained Melody (3:50)
6. September Song (4:35)
7. On the Sunny Side of the Street (2:36)
8. Moonlight in Vermont (3:26)
9. Don't Get Around Much Anymore (2:33)
10. Someone To Watch Over Me (4:03)

Total album length: 37 minutes

WILLIE NELSON
STARDUST

SUSANNA CLARK

38 "Live" Bullet

| • **Album sales:** 5,300,000 | • **Release date:** August 1976 |

It is rare for an artist to record a live album that then acts as the catalyst for newfound commercial success. But that is exactly what happened with Bob Seger and his Silver Bullet Band and their *"Live" Bullet* album, recorded at Detroit's Cobo Hall. While the American guitarist-singer had a decent enough following in his own backyard, it was the album's release in the summer of 1976 that boosted his career in his home country and brought him a wider audience abroad. In June 1976, Seger played in front of 50 people in a Chicago bar; three days later, he performed to 76,000 devoted fans in the Pontiac Silverdome outside Detroit.

While *"Live" Bullet* managed a modest Number 34 placing on the US Hot 100 and did not even chart in the UK, it nevertheless built slowly and gave an insight into Seger's bluesy, almost funky, approach to rock 'n' roll. Covers of songs such as Tina Turner's "Nutbush City Limits" and Van Morrison's "I've Been Working" are evidence of the funky side, while "Ramblin' Gamblin' Man" is pure American bar-room rock 'n' roll.

Number One singles:
None

Grammy Awards: None

Label: US & UK: Capitol

Recorded in: Live in Detroit, USA

Personnel:
Bob Seger
Drew Abbott
Alto Reed
Robyn Robbins
Chris Campbell
Charlie Allen Martin

Producers:
Bob Seger
Eddie "Punch" Andrews

1. Nutbush City Limits (4:37)
2. Travelin' Man (4:53)
3. Beautiful Loser (4:00)
4. Jody Girl (4:36)
5. I've Been Working (4:37)
6. Turn the Page (5:06)
7. U.M.C. (Upper Middle Class) (3:17)
8. Bo Diddley (5:47)
9. Ramblin' Gamblin' Man (3:01)
10. Heavy Music (8:14)
11. Katmandu (6:43)
12. Lookin' Back (2:36)
13. Get Out of Denver (5:21)
14. Let It Rock (8:29)

Total album length: 1 hour 11 minutes

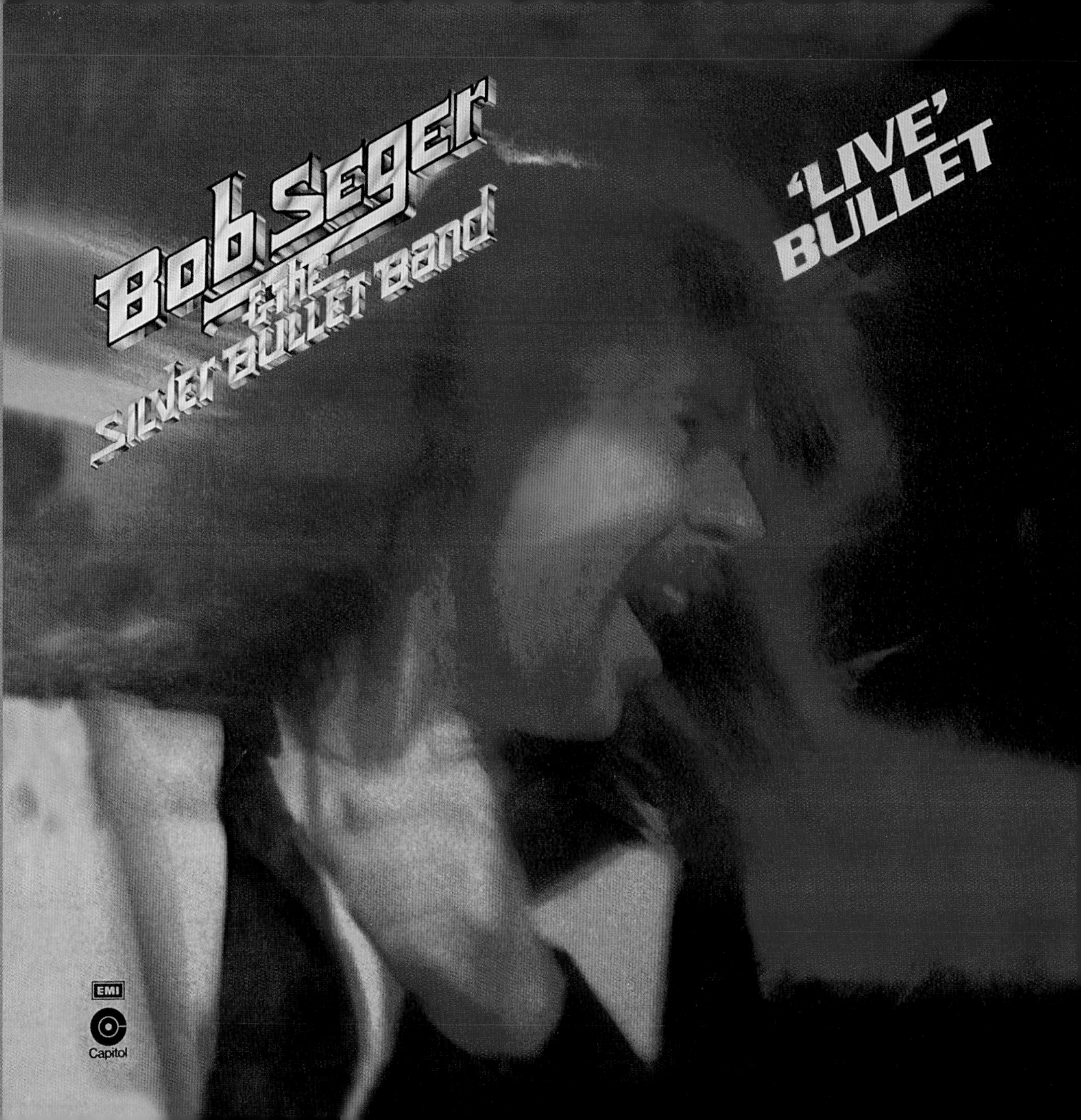

Bob Seger & the Silver Bullet Band

'LIVE' BULLET

Sleeve artwork by Roy Kohara and Thomas Weschler

EMI

Capitol

37 Stranger in Town

• **Album sales:** 6,050,000 | • **Release date:** May 1978

Gritty but big-hearted, Bob Seger was the sound of blue-collar America, detailing the lives of the common man through diner, roadhouse, and bar. With its raunchy, rhythmic rock, combined with a winning touch of sentimentality, *Stranger in Town* consolidated his growth from a huge local act in his native Detroit to a nationwide big draw. The album peaked at Number Four, and became his first Top 40 album in the UK, reaching 31. The album spent 110 weeks on the charts.

Seger's R&B-based rock takes on a more commercial sheen than on his previous album. "Still the Same" became a Top Five single in the US, as did the album's opener, "Hollywood Nights." Also, somewhat hidden away, was "We've Got Tonight," one of Seger's strongest songs and today his most covered.

Stranger in Town saw David Teegarden taking over from Charlie Allen Martin as drummer, while keyboardist Robyn Robins quit the Silver Bullet Band after the album's release.

Together with 1976's *Night Moves*, Seger had now set the path for the next decade, with several Top 10 hits, including his only Number One, "Shakedown," from 1987's *Beverly Hills Cop II* soundtrack.

"Old Time Rock and Roll" also re-entered the charts in 1983 after it was featured in the hit movie *Risky Business*, starring Tom Cruise.

Number One singles:
None

Grammy Awards: None

Label: US & UK: Capitol

Recorded in: California, USA

Personnel:
Bob Seger
Bill Payne
Alto Reed
Robyn Robins
David Teegarden
Drew Abbott
Chris Campbell

Producer:
Eddie "Punch" Andrews

1. **Hollywood Nights** (4:59)
2. **Still the Same** (3:18)
3. **Old Time Rock and Roll** (3:14)
4. **Till It Shines** (3:50)
5. **Feel Like a Number** (3:42)
6. **Ain't Got No Money** (4:11)
7. **We've Got Tonight** (4:38)
8. **Brave Strangers** (6:20)
9. **Famous Final Scene** (5:09)

Total album length: 39 minutes

Bob Seger AND THE Silver Bullet Band

Stranger in Town

Capitol
RECORDS

36 Night Moves

| • **Album sales:** 6,200,000 | • **Release date:** November 1976 |

Until *Night Moves,* Bob Seger was one of rock music's greatest underachievers, an artist with a growing live reputation—having made an impression with his *"Live" Bullet* live album—but never seemingly able to rise above cult status.

However, the release of *Night Moves,* and the title track in particular, dramatically turned around the fortunes of the Detroit-born musician, who found himself thrust into a "blue-collar" rock market already occupied by one of *Night Moves'* most important influences, Bruce Springsteen.

The album, which featured the Silver Bullet Band on one side and the Muscle Shoals Rhythm Section on the other, was the result of Seger's manager Eddie "Punch" Andrews hooking him up with Toronto-based producer Jack Richardson.

The title track came last for Seger, emerging so late during the album's recording that two of his band had already been sent home when it was cut in a 2:30 a.m. session. Inspired by the movie *American Graffiti,* the result was a coming-of-age classic that set the blueprint for the rest of Seger's career. The song returned the singer to the US Top 40 for the first time in eight years, peaking at Number Four on the Hot 100 in early 1977, while the album reached Number Eight.

Number One singles:
None

Grammy Awards: None

Label: US & UK: Capitol

Recorded in: Toronto, Canada

Producers:
Jack Richardson
Bob Seger
Eddie "Punch" Andrews

Personnel:
Bob Seger
Drew Abbott
Chris Campbell
Charlie Allen Martin
Rhonda Silver
Laurel Ward
Sharon Williams
Roger Hawkins
Pete Carr
Robin Robbins
Jerry Luck
Alto Reed
Barry Beckett
David Hood
Joe Miquelon
Doug Riley

1. **Rock & Roll Never Forgets** (3:52)
2. **Night Moves** (5:25)
3. **The Fire Down Below** (4:28)
4. **Sunburst** (5:13)
5. **Sunspot Baby** (4:38)
6. **Mainstreet** (3:43)
7. **Come To Poppa** (3:11)
8. **Ship of Fools** (3:24)
9. **Mary Lou** (2:56)

Total album length: 36 minutes

EMI

Capitol

Bob Seger & the Silver Bullet Band

NIGHT MOVES

35 The Cars

| • **Album sales:** 6,200,000 | • **Release date:** May 1978 |

The Cars took just 12 days to record their debut album, but with it created a classic that helped to open up American radio to new wave.

Against a backdrop of the likes of The Sex Pistols failing to make an impact on the US mainstream, this self-titled set captured some of the essence of punk, but presented a more radio-friendly sound that was pleasing to programmers.

The album's first three tracks alone, "Good Times Roll," "My Best Friend's Girl," and "Just What I Needed," remain FM rock staples as well as career highlights for the Boston band, whose label Elektra hooked them up with Queen producer Roy Thomas Baker to make this debut. Baker would go on to produce their next three albums as well. His Queen-like mark is evident throughout the album, which was recorded in London in early 1978, as is frontman Ric Ocasek's ability to write one catchy hook after another.

Released in May 1978, the album was an archetype slow-burner, taking another 10 months to reach its peak position of Number 18 in the US chart. By that time, The Cars had been named *Rolling Stone*'s new band of the year and had been nominated for a Grammy in the new artist category. The album went on to accumulate a chart run of 139 weeks.

Number One singles:
None

Grammy Awards: None

Label: US & UK: Elektra

Recorded in: London, UK

Personnel:
Ric Ocasek
Benjamin Orr
David Robinson
Elliot Easton
Greg Hawkes

Producer:
Roy Thomas Baker

1. **Good Times Roll** (3:44)
2. **My Best Friend's Girl** (3:44)
3. **Just What I Needed** (3:44)
4. **I'm In Touch With Your World** (3:31)
5. **Don't Cha Stop** (3:01)
6. **You're All I've Got Tonight** (4:13)
7. **Bye Bye Love** (4:14)
8. **Moving in Stereo** (5:15)
9. **All Mixed Up** (4:14)

Total album length: 35 minutes

THE CARS

Sleeve artwork by Johnny Lee, Ron Coro, and Elliot Gilbert

34 | Some Girls

| • **Album sales:** 6,200,000 | • **Release date:** June 1978 |

Having successfully sold R&B back to the Americans in the 1960s, The Rolling Stones' uncanny knack for successfully surfing musical trends reappeared with "Miss You," the opening track to 1978's *Some Girls*. A hypnotically gritty take on the disco craze, "Miss You," with its deeply funky bass line, caught the imagination of American record buyers, who propelled the single to the top of the US singles chart. The song reached Number Three in the UK.

Otherwise, *Some Girls*, which reached the top spot in the US album charts, Number Two in the UK, and spent an impressive 82 weeks on the charts, is a typical slice of Rolling Stones fare: "When the Whip Comes Down," "Respectable," and "Shattered" all feature the grinding guitar riffs that the band had come to make their own, while "Beast of Burden" is one of the Stones' best love songs. The country-and-western styled "Far Away Eyes" provides a change of pace.

The original version of the album cover, designed by Peter Corriston, featured the faces of famous actresses, but had to be reshot because the band had not secured permission.

In 2003, *Some Girls* was chosen as the 269th greatest album of all time by the editors of *Rolling Stone* magazine.

Number One singles:
US: "Miss You"

Grammy Awards: None

Label: US & UK: Rolling Stones

Recorded in: Paris, France

Personnel:
Mick Jagger
Keith Richards
Ron Wood
Bill Wyman
Charlie Watts
Ian McLagan

Producers:
The Glimmer Twins

1. Miss You (4:48)
2. When the Whip Comes Down (4:21)
3. Imagination (4:38)
4. Some Girls (4:36)
5. Lies (3:11)
6. Far Away Eyes (4:23)
7. Respectable (3:07)
8. Before They Make Me Run (3:25)
9. Beast of Burden (4:25)
10. Shattered (3:47)

Total album length: 40 minutes

Sleeve artwork by Peter Corriston

THE ROLLING STONES

Some Girls

Some Girls

Some Girls

$6.99

$6.99

$6.99

$6.99

$6.99

Some Girls

PERMA-STYLED WASH-N-WEAR

READY FOR INSTANT WEAR

Some Girls

STYLE No. TST-79
Lies - lies you dirty Jezebel
Why, why, why why don't you go to Hell?
MISS YOU $6.99

STYLE No PBF-79
Pretty Baby **FREEDOM**
100% CAREFREE WASH & WEAR
Some girls give me jewelry

STYLE No CT-79
Some GIRLS
RELAXED CURL

STYLE No TS-79
GEORGIE Girl
TAPERED BACK

AFRO
100% CAREFREE WASH & WEAR
Synthetic Japanese Cordelon

INSTANT BEAUTY

PERMA-STYLED

100% WASH & WEAR

READY FOR INSTANT WEAR

6 IN 1
FLIP UNDER or FLIP OUT

KOOL-N-LIGHT

Wash and Wear
French girls they want Cartier

LIGHT COOL AIRY—

Some Girls

Some Girls

Beast of Burden $7.99
STYLE No. DNY-89

Heavenly **BEAUTY** $7.99

STYLE No. NC-89
IMAGINATION $7.99

FarAwayEyes
Laughter, joy, and loneliness
and sex and sex and sex and sex

FREEDOM WIG
SOFT RELAXED CURLS
Some girls give me children

100% Synthetic Japanese MODACRYLIC

COOL-CAPLESS Comfortable

PERMA-STYLED

Miracle Fibre

NEVER NEED SETTING

Some Girls

KOOL-N-LIGHT

New Lovely You
Style No. MU-99

Some Girls

CAPLESS SKIN-TOP BEAU CATCHER $8.99

SHATTERED $8.99
STYLE No. LIC-99
Synthetic Japanese MODACRYLIC

BOY-CUT *Shorty* $8.99
STYLE No. LBC-99
Black girls just wanta get ...

`When the Whip Comes Down` $8.99

WIZ-WIG
SUPER FREEDOM
Italian girls want cars

100% MIRACLE FIBRE

BEAUTIFUL YOU in a few seconds

BEAUTIFUL YOU in a few seconds

NEVER NEED SETTING

PERMA-STYLED

PART CENTER RIGHT or LEFT

FLIP UNDER or FLIP OUT

STYLE No. SK-109
Some Girls

100% WASH & WEAR
STYLE No. SKGY-109
Before They Make Gups4
Me Run

DR. CORTIZONES' APPROVED
LIES Gups4

STYLE No RS-109
Skin-Crown $9.99

6 in 1
SOME GIRLS Style No. SKPB-109

33 All Things Must Pass

| • Album sales: 6,250,000 | • Release date: November 1970 |

George Harrison was overflowing with so much unreleased material from his Beatles days that when it came to his first, full solo album he had enough songs to fill four sides, plus have a third bonus disc. *All Things Must Pass* shows that, for Harrison, being unburdened of the constraints of the Fab Four allowed him to grow musically.

The album ranks among the best of The Beatles' solo releases. Songs include "Isn't It a Pity" and "My Sweet Lord," which made him the first Beatle to have a solo Number One single in both the UK and US. Its success, though, was eclipsed when Harrison lost a plagiarism suit over the song's similarities to the Chiffons' "He's So Fine," written by Ronnie Mack.

The album found Harrison surrounded by musical friends, among them Eric Clapton, Ringo Starr, and Billy Preston, while Bob Dylan is a songwriting contributor. Although an expensive boxed triple set, the album replaced *Led Zeppelin III* as the US Number One in January 1971 and stayed there for seven weeks.

Number One singles:
US & UK: "My Sweet Lord"

Grammy Awards: None

Label: US & UK: Apple

Recorded in: London, UK

Personnel:
George Harrison
Ringo Starr
Jim Gordon
Alan White
Klaus Voormann

Carl Radle
Gary Wright
Bobby Whitlock
Billy Preston
Gary Brooker
Pete Drake
Eric Clapton
Dave Mason
Bobby Keys
Badfinger

Producers:
George Harrison
Phil Spector

1. I'd Have You Anytime (2:57)
2. My Sweet Lord (4:57)
3. Wah-Wah (5:35)
4. Isn't It a Pity (7:08)
5. What Is Life (4:22)
6. If Not For You (3:29)
7. Behind That Locked Door (3:05)
8. Let It Down (4:57)
9. Run of the Mill (2:51)
10. Beware of Darkness (3:48)
11. Apple Scruffs (3:04)
12. Ballad of Sir Frankie Crisp (Let It Roll) (3:46)
13. Awaiting on You All (2:45)
14. All Things Must Pass (3:44)
15. I Dig Love (4:54)
16. Art of Dying (3:37)
17. Isn't It a Pity (version two) (4:45)
18. Hear Me Lord (5:48)
19. It's Johnny's Birthday (0:49)
20. Plug Me In (3:18)
21. I Remember Jeep (8:05)
22. Thanks For the Pepperoni (5:32)
23. Out of the Blue (11:13)

Total album length:
1 hour 44 minutes

GEORGE HARRISON
ALL THINGS MUST PASS

32 | In Through the Out Door

| • **Album sales:** 6,350,000 | • **Release date:** August 1979 |

Led Zeppelin's eighth studio album proved to be the band's last. Following recording, they embarked on a brief tour across Europe in 1979 and a series of dates at the English country estate Knebworth—the band's first UK gigs for four years. Any further activity was stopped in its tracks by the death of drummer John Bonham the following year.

The album, recorded by Zeppelin in Polar Studio in Stockholm, is a hit and miss affair: It opens grandly enough with a typically Zeppelin track, the sweeping and anthemic "In the Evening." "Carouselambra" and "I'm Gonna Crawl" all have echoes of material from the days of *Physical Graffiti*, but elsewhere the band is heard mixing up styles, and experimenting with

new instruments as well. The album's standout track, and one of the first Zeppelin songs to feature synthesizers, is "All My Love."

Despite carping from critics, fans lapped it up, sending the album to the summits of both US and UK album charts on its release. *In Through the Out Door* remained in the UK charts for 16 weeks and in the US charts for 28 weeks. It has been suggested that the title might be a sexual innuendo.

The original LP record of this album featured an unusual gimmick. It had an outer sleeve that was made to look like a plain brown paper bag, and the sleeve proper featured black and white line artwork that, if washed with a wet brush, would (permanently) become fully colored.

Number One singles:
None

Grammy Awards: None

Label: US & UK: Swan Song

Recorded in: Stockholm, Sweden

Personnel:
Robert Plant
Jimmy Page
John Bonham
John Paul Jones

Producers:
Jimmy Page
Peter Grant

1. **In the Evening** (6:50)
2. **South Bound Saurez** (4:14)
3. **Fool in the Rain** (6:13)
4. **Hot Dog** (3:17)
5. **Carouselambra** (10:34)
6. **All My Love** (5:56)
7. **I'm Gonna Crawl** (5:30)

Total album length: 42 minutes

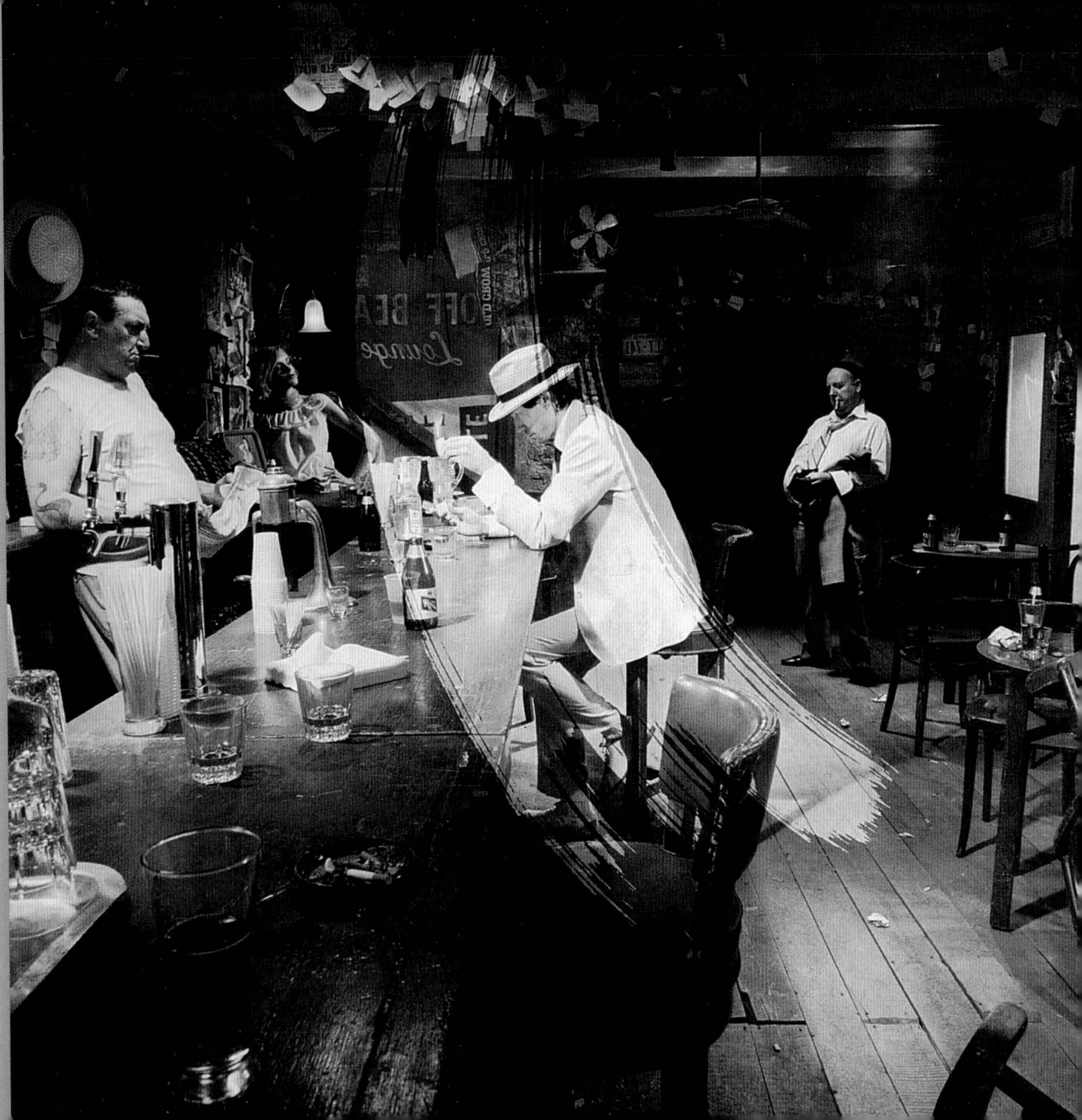

Sleeve artwork by Hipgnosis

31 Led Zeppelin III

| • **Album sales:** 6,500,000 | • **Release date:** October 1970 |

*L*ed Zeppelin III, the band's third album, was recorded in Zeppelin's mobile studio at Headley Grange in Hampshire, UK. The album added acoustic and folk rock elements to Zeppelin's rock and blues repertoire, which also helped endear the band to progressive rock fans. It repeated the success of its predecessor, *II*, by topping both the US and UK charts at the end of 1970, and by remaining in the UK charts for more than 40 weeks and the US charts for 19 weeks.

Familiar enough territory is covered in the opening "Immigrant Song," which has all the mystical sweep and grandeur that Led Zeppelin fans had come to expect, and reached Number 16 in the *Billboard* Hot 100. Blues fans are admirably catered to on the album's pivotal cut,

"Since I've Been Loving You." Other tracks, such as "Friends" and "Celebration Day," show that the band had lost none of its ability to deliver bombastic rock. Yet *III* also proved that Led Zeppelin had considerably more to offer; notably, a deeply held affection for folk music, as displayed on the traditional song "Gallows Pole." The lilting "Tangerine" and "That's the Way" also illustrate that Zeppelin possessed the courage to go "unplugged," years before anyone had heard of MTV.

The original vinyl edition was packaged in a gatefold sleeve with a novelty cover. A rotatable paper disc covered with pictures of the band members was visible through artfully positioned holes on the cover.

Number One singles:	**Personnel:**
None	Robert Plant
	Jimmy Page
Grammy Awards:	John Bonham
None	John Paul Jones
Label: US & UK: Atlantic	**Producers:**
	Jimmy Page
Recorded in: Hampshire, UK	Peter Grant

1. Immigrant Song (2:23)
2. Friends (3:54)
3. Celebration Day (3:28)
4. Since I've Been Loving You (7:24)
5. Out on the Tiles (4:05)
6. Gallows Pole (4:56)
7. Tangerine (2:57)
8. That's the Way (5:37)
9. Bron-Y-Aur Stomp (4:16)
10. Hats Off To (Roy) Harper (3:42)

Total album length: 38 minutes

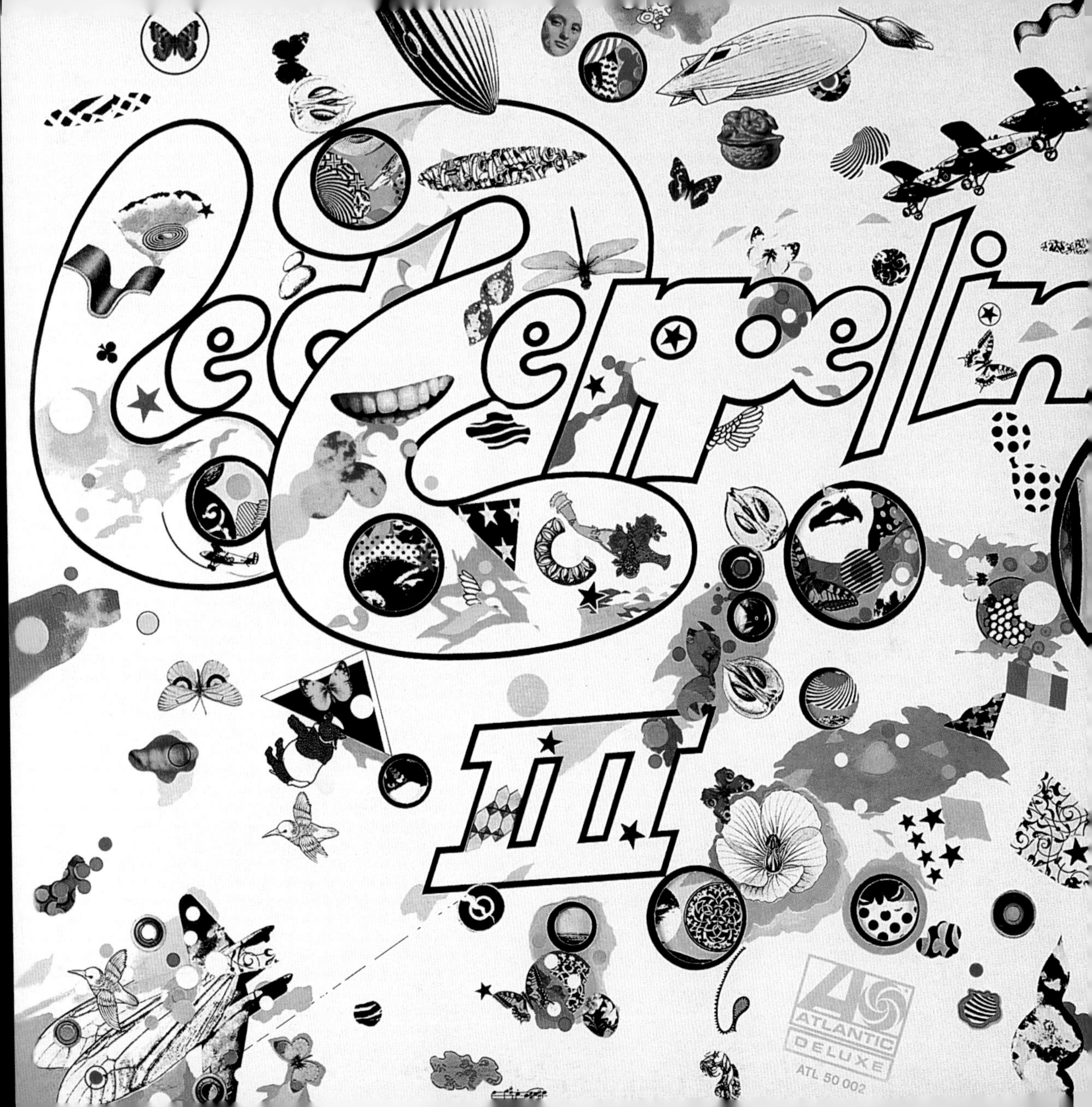

Sleeve artwork by Zacron

30 Born To Run

| • **Album sales:** 6,600,000 | • **Release date:** September 1975 |

After his first two albums had sold disappointingly, Springsteen revised the lineup of his backing group, the E Street Band, and toured the country playing three-hour sets while writing new material. His third album, *Born To Run*, with its moving theme of desolation and redemption, firmly established the New Jersey-born songwriter's reputation. The title track to the album brought Springsteen to the attention of a wide audience on both sides of the Atlantic.

Born To Run, recorded at the Record Plant in New York, was the first of Springsteen's albums to enter the charts in both the US, where it reached Number Three, and the UK, where it achieved a more modest Number 17 placing. The record sold more than 700,000 copies within weeks of its release in the US. It reached gold status on October 8 that year and was to become the first album to be awarded the US music industry's new platinum certification.

Two singles from the album made it into the US Hot 100, "Born To Run" reaching Number 23 and "Tenth Avenue Freeze Out" reaching Number 83, although neither achieved a high placing in the UK. The album's success saw Springsteen on the front covers of *Time* and *Newsweek*. John Landau, one of the producers, later became Springsteen's manager.

Number One singles:
None

Grammy Awards:
None

Label: US: Columbia;
UK: CBS

Recorded in: New York,
USA

Producers:
Jon Landau
Bruce Springsteen
Mike Appel

Personnel:
Bruce Springsteen
Stevie van Zandt
Danny Federici
Roy Bittan
Garry Tallent
Max Weinberg
Clarence Clemons
Randy Brecker
Michael Brecker
Dave Sanborn
Wayne Andre
Ernest "Boom" Carter
David Sancious
Suki Lehav

1. **Thunder Road** (4:50)
2. **Tenth Avenue Freeze Out** (3:11)
3. **Night** (3:01)
4. **Backstreets** (6:30)
5. **Born To Run** (4:30)
6. **She's the One** (4:30)
7. **Meeting Across the River** (3:19)
8. **Jungleland** (9:33)

Total album length: 39 minutes

BRUCE
SPRINGSTEEN
BORN TO RUN

Sleeve artwork by John Berg, Andy Engel, and Eric Meola

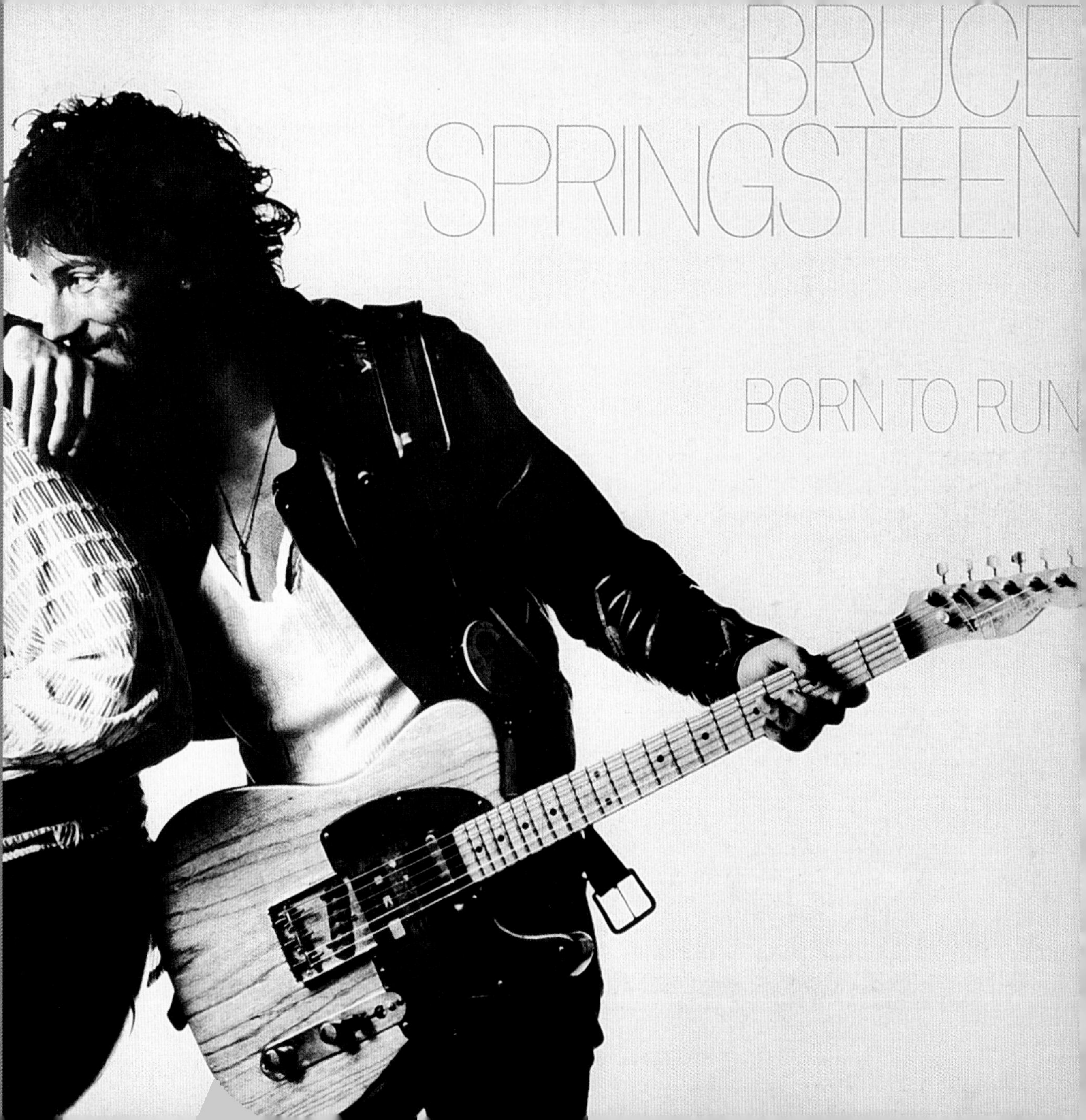

29 Dirty Deeds Done Dirt Cheap

| • **Album sales:** 6,750,000 | • **Release date:** December 1976 |

Technically AC/DC's third studio album, *Dirty Deeds Done Dirt Cheap* is a no-nonsense bar-room rock album, full of vitality and illustrating the band's willingness to ignore then-current musical fashion and produce nine simple goodtime rock and roll tracks. It was produced by Harry Vanda and George Young.

Songs like the title track, "Love at First Feel," "Big Balls," and "Ride On" leave little to the imagination and merely serve to confirm any doubters that AC/DC do not care what non-believers think about their material. The band had by the album's release created a fanatical following in their new base, the UK, where their arrival from their home in Australia coincided with the punk rock explosion. While AC/DC were not punk, their hard, fast, loud music enabled them to ride the shirt tails of the movement—and outlast it. It is also a testament to the talents of frontman Bon Scott, whose vocals on the album are typically uncompromising.

The album was turned down by the US record company and was deprived of a US release until after Scott's death in 1980, when American fans had already heard the singer who had replaced him, ex-Geordie frontman Brian Johnson. The album eventually hit Number Three in the US in the spring of 1981; it had reached Number 47 in the UK some five years earlier.

Number One singles:
None

Grammy Awards: None

Label: US & UK: Atlantic

Recorded in: Sydney, Australia

Personnel:
Bon Scott
Angus Young
Malcolm Young
Phil Rudd
Mark Evans

Producers:
Harry Vanda
George Young

1. **Dirty Deeds Done Dirt Cheap** (3:46)
2. **Love at First Feel** (3:05)
3. **Big Balls** (2:39)
4. **Rocker** (2:46)
5. **Problem Child** (5:43)
6. **There's Gonna Be Some Rockin'** (3:14)
7. **Ain't No Fun (Waitin' Round To Be a Millionaire)** (6:57)
8. **Ride On** (5:47)
9. **Squealer** (5:12)

Total album length: 41 minutes

AC/DC

Dirty Deeds Done Dirt Cheap

Sleeve artwork by Hipgnosis and Paul Candy

28 Double Vision

| • **Album sales:** 7,050,000 | • **Release date:** July 1978 |

Like other "supergroup" acts to have hit the motherlode with their first album, Foreigner's follow-up record to their hugely successful debut was more of the same AOR formula, although this did not stop the band fretting about reproducing such a mega-selling success.

While their fears were understandable, the album went on to outsell its predecessor, which was still on the charts, delivering more radio-friendly rock-pop. The singles "Hot Blooded" and "Double Vision" reached Numbers Three and Two in the US respectively, confirming the band's status as one of the more successful rock acts around.

The band was yet to make a significant impact on the other side of the Atlantic—"Double Vision" was not released as a single in the UK until almost a year after the album. The LP reached Number Three on the US album chart, but only scraped into the Top 40 in the UK, peaking at Number 32.

This release also marked the departure of bassist Ed Gagliardi, who was replaced by ex-Roxy Music Rick Wills, a childhood friend of Pink Floyd's Dave Gilmour.

The band wrote the song "Double Vision" after seeing New York Rangers goalie John Davidson get knocked out during the 1977 Stanley Cup playoffs.

Number One singles:
None

Grammy Awards: None

Label: US & UK: Atlantic

Recorded in: New York, USA

Personnel:
Lou Gramm
Mick Jones
Ian McDonald
Al Greenwood
Ed Gagliardi
Dennis Elliott

Producers:
Ken Olson
Mick Jones
Ian McDonald

1. Hot Blooded (4:28)
2. Blue Morning, Blue Day (3:12)
3. You're All I Am (3:24)
4. Back Where You Belong (3:15)
5. Love Has Taken Its Toll (3:31)
6. Double Vision (3:44)
7. Tramontane (3:56)
8. I Have Waited So Long (4:07)
9. Lonely Children (3:37)
10. Spellbinder (4:55)

Total album length: 38 minutes

FOREIGNER

DOUBLE VISION

27 Wish You Were Here

| • **Album sales:** 7,100,000 | • **Release date:** September 1975 |

Another marathon session of recording activity—seven months—again at London's Abbey Road Studios went into producing *Wish You Were Here*, Pink Floyd's follow-up to their highly regarded *Dark Side of the Moon*. During recording, the band came close to breakup (both Roger Waters and Nick Mason were splitting from their wives at the time), but many critics now regard the album as one of Pink Floyd's best.

It opens with a clear homage to founding member—and, at the time, institutionalized—Syd Barrett on "Shine On You Crazy Diamond (Parts I–V)." The album then takes the listener on a sort of aural spaceship ride, with heavy use of synthesizers and futuristic sound effects, as well as more conventional instruments such as acoustic guitars and piano.

Signs that bassist and lyricist Roger Waters was becoming exasperated with the whole music business—and perhaps with his fellow band members, too—also take shape on the record: In "Have a Cigar," he has a record company executive saying "The band is just fantastic/that is really what I think/By the way, which one's Pink?"

Wish You Were Here scored a Number One in the album charts on both sides of the Atlantic, only the second time that the band had topped the chart in their home market.

Number One singles: None

Grammy Awards: None

Label: US: Columbia;
UK: Harvest

Recorded in: London, UK

Personnel:
Dave Gilmour
Roger Waters
Rick Wright
Nick Mason

Producers:
Pink Floyd

1. **Shine On You Crazy Diamond (Parts I–V)** (13:30)
2. **Welcome to the Machine** (7:26)
3. **Have a Cigar** (5:08)
4. **Wish You Were Here** (5:40)
5. **Shine On You Crazy Diamond (Parts VI–IX)** (12:22)

Total album length: 44 minutes

Pink Floyd

Sleeve artwork by Hipgnosis and George Hardie

26 Don't Look Back

| • **Album sales:** 7,150,000 | • **Release date:** August 1978 |

Following their sensationally successful 17-million-selling debut album would have been tough for Boston no matter what, but band founder and studio boffin Tom Scholz's endless tinkerings as he beavered away at his aptly named Hideaway Studio soon began to grate on his label bosses. Tension was building between the producer-band leader and then-CBS president Walter Yetnikoff; when tapes were finally delivered, Epic opted to rush-release *Don't Look Back*. The result is a virtual retread of its predecessor, right down to the futuristic sleeve.

Ever the studio perfectionist, Scholz made sure every beat was spot on, every hook just right, and every chord nailed with precision. Despite this, he would later claim that the album was only half-finished. It still sold well, hitting the Number One spot in the US with more than seven million sales, and even managing a higher chart position in the UK—Number Nine—than the band's debut. Meanwhile, a Number Four berth in the singles charts with the title track kept things ticking over in the US. In all, the album spent 35 weeks on the charts.

Despite the album's success, Scholz vowed never to release an album again before he was ready. He was true to his word—it would be another eight years before the band produced their third album.

Number One singles:
None

Grammy Awards: None

Label: US & UK: Epic

Recorded in: Boston, USA

Personnel:
Tom Scholz
Fran Sheehan
Barry Goudreau
Bradley Delp
Sib Hashain

Producer:
Tom Scholz

1. **Don't Look Back** (5:58)
2. **The Journey** (1:46)
3. **It's Easy** (4:27)
4. **A Man I'll Never Be** (6:38)
5. **Feelin' Satisfied** (4:12)
6. **Party** (4:07)
7. **Used To Bad News** (2:57)
8. **Don't Be Afraid** (3:50)

Total album length: 34 minutes

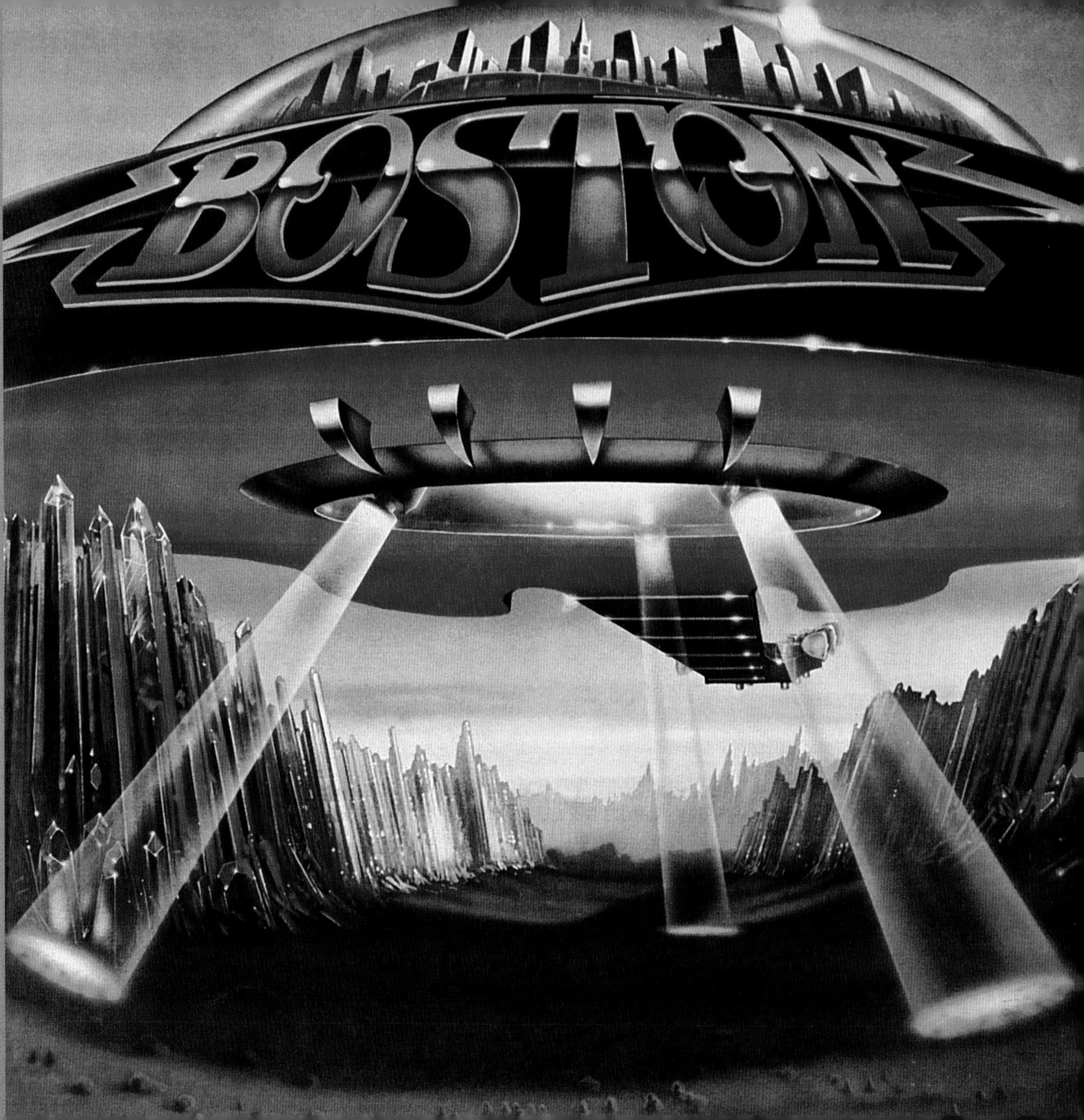

Sleeve artwork by Gary Norman

25 52nd Street

| • **Album sales:** 7,150,000 | • **Release date:** October 1978 |

For *52nd Street*, Billy Joel stuck wisely to the mid-tempo songs and ballads that had broken him through with his previous album *The Stranger*. The album, which was produced, like its predecessor, by Phil Ramone, explored a jazzier feel to Joel, with a guest spot for trumpet great Freddie Hubbard, but the high caliber of the sure-fire hits present on the album ensured that the singer-pianist was not about to deviate from a winning formula that had turned him into one of the biggest stars in the US.

The thumping but characteristically melodic single "My Life" gave Joel his biggest US hit since "Just the Way You Are," selling a million and reaching Number Three in January 1979. This was followed into the Top 40 by "Big Shot" and "Honesty." On the song "Until the Night," Joel pays homage to Phil Spector and, in particular, the Righteous Brothers.

After Joel's frustration at the all-conquering *Saturday Night Fever* preventing *The Stranger* reaching Number One, this follow-up took just three weeks after its October 1978 release to give him a first US chart-topper. Residing there for eight weeks and spending 76 weeks on the charts, it was declared Album of the Year at the February 1980 Grammy Awards and went on to become the first-ever album issued on CD.

Number One singles:
None

Grammy Awards: Best Pop Vocal Performance, Male; Album of the Year

Label: US: Columbia; UK: CBS

Recorded in: New York, USA

Producer: Phil Ramone

Personnel:
Billy Joel
Doug Stegmeyer
Liberty DeVitto
Ralph McDoanld
Mike Mainieri
Richie Cannata
Steve Khan
Hugh McCracken
David Spinozza
Eric Gale
Dave Brown
Russell Javors
Robert Freedman
George Marge
Freddie Hubbard

1. **Big Shot (4:03)**
2. **Honesty (3:53)**
3. **My Life (4:44)**
4. **Zanzibar (5:13)**
5. **Stiletto (4:42)**
6. **Rosalinda's Eyes (4:41)**
7. **Half a Mile Away (4:08)**
8. **Until the Night (6:35)**
9. **52nd Street (5:04)**

Total album length: 40 minutes

Billy Joel

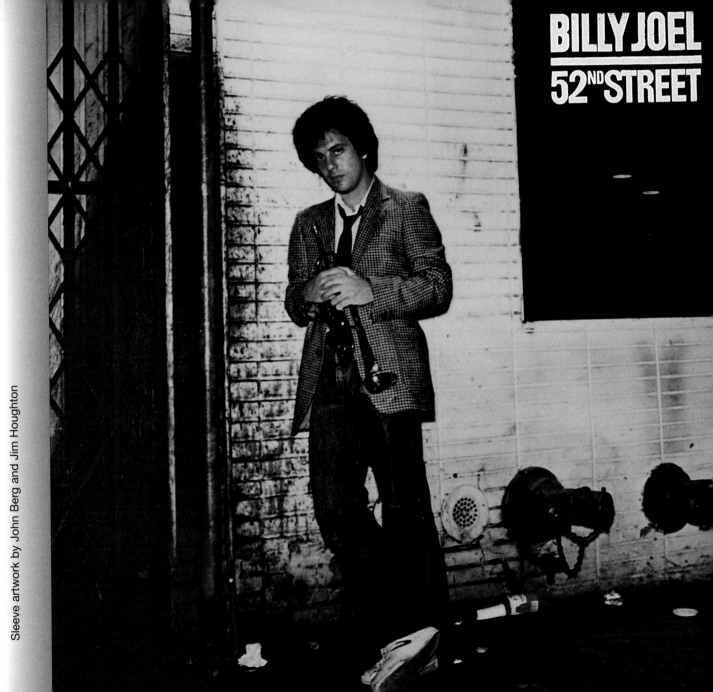

BILLY JOEL
52ND STREET

24 The Long Run

| • **Album sales:** 7,150,000 | • **Release date:** September 1979 |

Follow-up to the hugely successful *Hotel California*, *The Long Run* took a reported three years to complete, but, despite the amount of time expended on putting it together, it was never in with a chance of matching its illustrious and mega-selling predecessor.

Although the album sold millions and spawned hit singles in "Heartache Tonight," the title track, and the soft rock ballad "I Can't Tell You Why," it had considerably less of the creative spark of *Hotel California*, and, for those prepared to look for them, the signs were starting to appear that all was not heading in the right direction for the band. Don Henley's artistic stamp was not in much evidence, unlike on *Hotel California*, with the exception of the title track and the album's closer, "The Sad Café." Long-time bassist Randy Meisner had left to pursue a solo career and was replaced by ex-Poco Timothy B. Schmit. Joe Walsh's "In the City" might not even have been a song destined for an Eagles' record, having already appeared on a different recording as a Walsh solo on the soundtrack to the movie *The Warriors*.

Still, all of this didn't prevent the album from topping the US charts, spending 57 weeks on the charts, and reaching Number Four in the UK. *The Long Run* was certified platinum in January 1980, less than four months after its release.

Number One singles:
US: "Heartache Tonight"

Grammy Awards: Best Rock Vocal Performance by a Duo or Group

Label: US & UK: Asylum

Recorded in: Florida, USA

Personnel:
Don Henley
Glenn Frey
Joe Walsh
Timothy B. Schmit
Don Felder

Producer:
Bill Szymczyk

1. The Long Run (3:43)
2. I Can't Tell You Why (4:55)
3. In the City (3:45)
4. Disco Strangler (2:45)
5. King of Hollywood (6:28)
6. Heartache Tonight (4:26)
7. Those Shoes (4:54)
8. Teenage Jail (3:44)
9. The Greeks Don't Want No Freaks (2:20)
10. The Sad Café (5:35)

Total album length: 42 minutes

EAGLES
THE LONG RUN

Sleeve artwork by Kosh and Jim Shea

23 Running on Empty

| • Album sales: 7,250,000 | • Release date: January 1978 |

Entering something of a creative lull following a run of sterling albums—his eponymous debut, *For Everyman, Late For The Sky*, and *The Pretender*—*Running on Empty* was regarded by many as lacking ambition, but was nevertheless Jackson Browne's most commercially successful of his career to date. It peaked at Number Three in the US and reached Number 28 in the UK.

Browne had exhausted himself emotionally on previous records, laying his soul bare, and the album's title suggests that he was indeed close to the edge. Although many of the songs were recorded onstage or in hotel rooms while touring, it is an album about being on the road,

rather than a genuinely "live" performance album. Titles such as "The Road," "Cocaine," and "The Load-Out"—an homage to his road crew—leave relatively little to the imagination.

With two hits in the US—"The Load-Out/Stay" and the title track—*Running on Empty* served Browne well. His heartfelt introspection is called upon on "Love Needs a Heart," an accessible lilting ballad very much in the Browne mold, while one of the album's highlights is Danny Kortchmar's "Shaky Town."

Number One singles:
None

Grammy Awards: None

Label: US & UK: Asylum

Recorded in: Various locations, USA

Personnel:
Jackson Browne
Leland Sklar
Russell Kunkel
David Lindley
Craig Doerge
Danny Kortchmar
Doug Hayward
Rosemary Butler

Producer:
Jackson Browne

1. Running on Empty (5:27)
2. The Road (4:50)
3. Rosie (3:41)
4. You Love the Thunder (3:56)
5. Cocaine (4:54)
6. Shaky Town (3:40)
7. Love Needs a Heart (3:30)
8. Nothing But Time (3:36)
9. The Load-Out (5:35)
10. Stay (3:22)

Total album length: 42 minutes

22 Déjà Vu

| • **Album sales:** 7,350,000 | • **Release date:** March 1970 |

David Crosby, Stephen Stills, and ex-Hollies Graham Nash had seen their eponymous debut album hit the Top 10 of the Hot 100 in the summer of 1969, and they had been named Best New Artist of the Year at that year's Grammy Awards. But it was when they were joined by ex-Buffalo Springfield guitarist Neil Young and recorded *Déjà Vu* that the ensemble really took off. The album topped the US Hot 100 and hit Number Five in the UK.

The record, with its lyrical content and alternating styles, caught the counterculture vibe of the time. There was much, too, to be admired in the band's intricate vocal harmonies, jangling acoustic guitars, and achingly beautiful songs, none more so than Young's "Helpless."

Young, whose arrival appears to have galvanized the band's performance, also contributed the pensive but no less lovely "Country Girl." Graham Nash's countrified exhortation "Teach Your Children" hit the Number 16 spot on the chart, and "Our House," also by Nash, managed Number 30.

One of the album's highlights is Stills' rendition of Joni Mitchell's "Woodstock," the single of which reached Number 11 in the US charts. Crosby, Stills, Nash and Young had performed at the Woodstock Festival the previous year.

Number One singles:
None

Grammy Awards: None

Label: US & UK: Atlantic

Recorded in:
Los Angeles, USA

Personnel:
David Crosby
Graham Nash
Stephen Stills
Neil Young
Dallas Taylor
Greg Reeves
Jerry Garcia
John Sebastian

Producers:
Crosby, Stills, Nash
& Young

1. Carry On (4:27)
2. Teach Your Children (2:55)
3. Almost Cut My Hair (4:31)
4. Helpless (3:40)
5. Woodstock (3:56)
6. Déjà Vu (4:14)
7. Our House (3:01)
8. 4 + 20 (2:08)
9. Country Girl (5:14)
10. Everybody I Love You (2:21)

Total album length: 36 minutes

Crosby, Stills, Nash & Young
Dallas Taylor & Greg Reeves

Déjà vu

Sleeve artwork by Gary Burden and Henry Diltz

21 Highway To Hell

| • **Album sales:** 7,350,000 | • **Release date:** August 1979 |

The riff to the opener and title track of *Highway To Hell* is perhaps the best in rock 'n' roll, topped only by the opener and title track to the band's subsequent work, *Back In Black*. AC/DC's sixth studio set, *Highway To Hell* was their first to be produced by "Mutt" Lange and the last to feature frontman Bon Scott. By far their most popular album at the time of its release, *Highway To Hell* expanded AC/DC's audience considerably. Bon Scott's death from alcohol poisoning in London six months after the record's release was all the more poignant since the album scored the success in the US that the band had long been seeking. It opened the door for the expatriate Scottish rockers to make the leap from club gigs in their adopted Australia,

and later in the UK, to the big time in the US. The music is typically uncompromising AC/DC material: hard rock songs such as "Touch Too Much," "Get It Hot," "Love Hungry Man," and, of course, the title track, leave few in any doubt that here was a band who relished having a good time. The album's success in the UK—a Number Eight placing—was less surprising than its Number 17 in the US.

The popularity of *Highway To Hell* paved the way for the multi-million selling album *Back In Black* a year later—still one of the biggest-selling records of all time in America—and a 1981 release in the US for the 1976-recorded *Dirty Deeds Done Dirt Cheap*.

Number One singles:
None

Grammy Awards: None

Label: US & UK: Atlantic

Recorded in: London, UK

Personnel:
Bon Scott
Angus Young
Malcolm Young
Phil Rudd
Cliff Williams

Producer:
Robert John "Mutt" Lange

1. Highway To Hell (3:28)
2. Girls Got Rhythm (3:23)
3. Walk All Over You (5:10)
4. Touch Too Much (4:26)
5. Beating Around the Bush (3:55)
6. Shot Down In Flames (3:22)
7. Get It Hot (2:34)
8. If You Want Blood (You've Got It) (4:36)
9. Love Hungry Man (4:17)
10. Night Prowler (6:27)

Total album length: 41 minutes

AC/DC

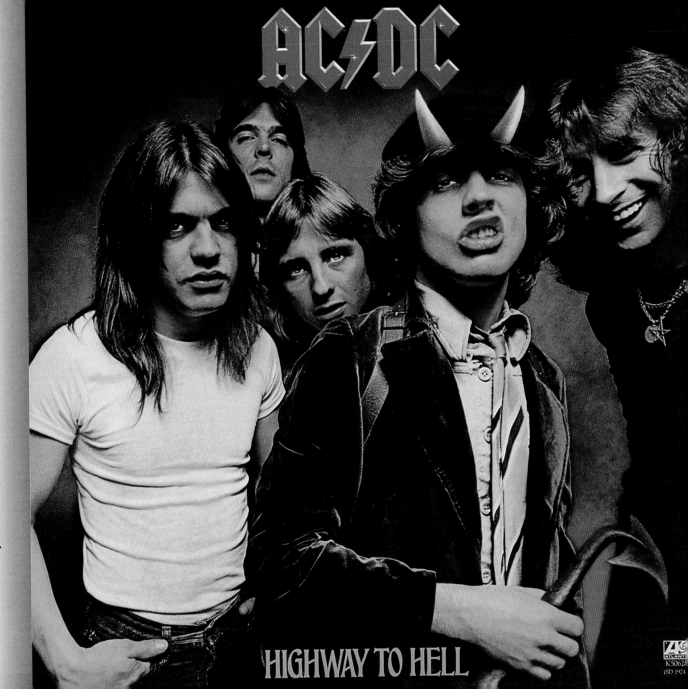

AC/DC

HIGHWAY TO HELL

K5062
SD 19
ATLANT

20 Frampton Comes Alive!

| • **Album sales:** 8,150,000 | • **Release date:** January 1976 |

English rock musician Peter Frampton was so determined to crack the US that by the mid-1970s he had thrown himself headlong into an exhausting tour schedule of around 200 dates a year.

The singer-guitarist's work paid off beyond his wildest dreams as his double album *Frampton Comes Alive!* became not only a Number One album in the US, but set an all-time sales benchmark for a live album release.

On the back of four moderately successful solo outings, Frampton viewed this live set, capturing him at the Winterland Ballroom in San Francisco, as a useful exercise in summarizing his solo career. What it did instead was propel him to superstardom, albeit momentarily.

The album's sound was made highly distinctive by a voicebox guitar technique in which Frampton made his guitar "speak" by filtering it through a microphone. It was showcased most memorably on the US Top 10 smash "Show Me the Way."

This album shattered the sales record of Carole King's *Tapestry* and hit Number One in the US in April 1976. Frampton's record stood until 1978, when the Bee Gees (and others) broke it with the soundtrack to the movie *Saturday Night Fever*. In the UK it managed a Number Six placing.

Number One singles:
None

Grammy Awards: None

Label: US & UK: A&M

Recorded in: San Francisco, USA

Personnel:
Peter Frampton
Bob Mayo
Stanley Sheldon
John Siomos

Producer:
Peter Frampton

1. Something's Happening (5:40)
2. Doobie Wah (5:34)
3. Show Me the Way (4:34)
4. It's a Plain Shame (4:36)
5. All I Wanna Be (Is By Your Side) (3:25)
6. Wind of Change (2:45)
7. Baby, I Love Your Way (4:37)
8. I Wanna Go To the Sun (7:14)
9. Penny For Your Thoughts (1:22)
10. (I'll Give You) Money (5:36)
11. Shine On (3:34)
12. Jumpin' Jack Flash (7:52)
13. Lines On My Face (7:02)
14. Do You Feel Like We Do (14:15)

Total album length: 78 minutes

Frampton Comes Alive!

Sleeve artwork by Roland Young and Stan Evenson

19 Toys in the Attic

| • **Album sales:** 8,250,000 | • **Release date:** April 1975 |

Seen by many as America's answer to The Rolling Stones, not least due to the image pushed to the fore by singer Steve Tyler and guitarist Joe Perry and the band's obvious enjoyment as they reveled in the fast lane of rock 'n' roll, Aerosmith's third album confirmed their status as the top live and recorded rock act of the day, at least in their homeland.

Recorded at the Record Plant in New York, and produced by Jack Douglas, *Toys in the Attic* was an immediate success. Tracks such as the epic "Sweet Emotion," the Zeppelin-esque "Round and Round," the blues-oriented "Adam's Apple," and the big-band boogie number "Big Ten Inch Record" combined the band's musical rock 'n' blues influence with an overtly upfront approach to sex.

In the US, the single "Toys in the Attic" stormed the Hot 100, peaking at Number 11, but in the UK, in the grip of the early days of the punk revolution, the record fell on stony ground.

The album is perhaps best known now for featuring the first real crossover song in rock in the form of "Walk This Way," which was remodeled to such great effect by rap act Run DMC 11 years later, doing much to rekindle interest in the band. It is one of the few songs in history that has charted in two decades.

Number One singles:
None

Grammy Awards: None

Label: US: Columbia;
UK: CBS

Recorded in: New York,
USA

Personnel:
Steve Tyler
Joe Perry
Tom Hamilton
Brad Whitford
Joey Kramer

Producer:
Jack Douglas

1. **Toys in the Attic** (3:06)
2. **Uncle Salty** (4:10)
3. **Adam's Apple** (4:33)
4. **Walk This Way** (3:41)
5. **Big Ten Inch Record** (2:16)
6. **Sweet Emotion** (4:34)
7. **No More No More** (4:34)
8. **Round and Round** (5:03)
9. **You See Me Crying** (5:12)

Total album length: 37 minutes

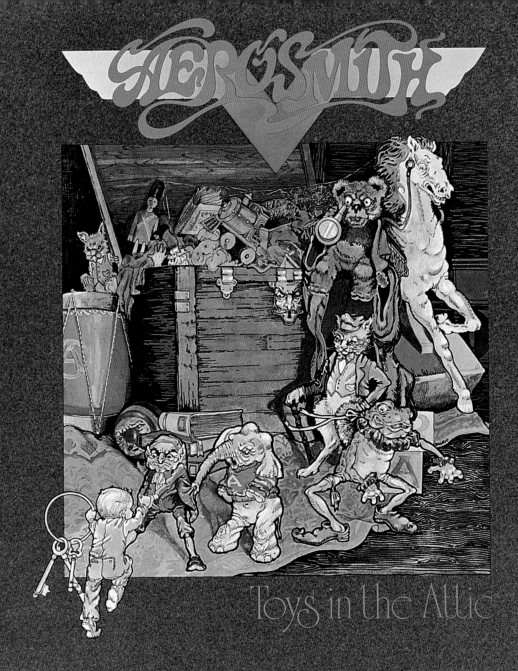

AEROSMITH

Toys in the Attic

18 Goodbye Yellow Brick Road

| • **Album sales:** 8,350,000 | • **Release date:** October 1973 |

Originally intended as a single album, by the time Elton John had finished recording tracks for *Goodbye Yellow Brick Road* it was clear—to him at any rate—that only a double LP would suffice. Yet initially he was concerned that his fans would balk at having to pay more than they were used to for his music. He needn't have worried: The album topped both US and UK charts and saw four singles, including the title track, all hit the upper reaches of both countries' charts. "Bennie and the Jets" was a Number One in the US.

While the instrumental opener "Funeral For a Friend" and "Saturday Night's Alright For Fighting" are musical standout tracks, the album also proved to be a tour de force for John's lyricist partner Bernie Taupin on such classics as the title track and "Candle in the Wind," a tribute to Marilyn Monroe.

Recorded at Château d'Hérouville outside Paris, where John had recorded *Honky Château* and *Don't Shoot Me I'm Only the Piano Player*, the sessions were completed in just three weeks.

Number One singles:
US: "Bennie and the Jets"
(UK: unreleased as A-side)

Grammy Awards:
None

Label: US: MCA;
UK: DJM

Recorded in: Paris,
France

Personnel:
Elton John
Dee Murray
Davy Johnstone
Nigel Olson
David Hentschel
Del Newman
Ray Cooper
Kiki Dee
Prince Rhino

Producer:
Gus Dudgeon

1. Funeral For a Friend/Love Lies Bleeding (11:09)
2. Candle in the Wind (3:49)
3. Bennie and the Jets (5:23)
4. Goodbye Yellow Brick Road (3:13)
5. This Song Has No Title (2:23)
6. Grey Seal (4:00)
7. Jamaica Jerk-Off (3:38)
8. I've Seen That Movie Too (5:58)
9. Sweet Painted Lady (3:54)
10. The Ballad of Danny Bailey (1909–34) (4:23)
11. Dirty Little Girl (5:01)
12. All the Girls Love Alice (5:09)
13. Your Sister Can't Twist (But She Can Rock & Roll) (2:42)
14. Saturday Night's Alright For Fighting (4:53)
15. Roy Roger (4:08)
16. Social Disease (3:43)
17. Harmony (2:46)

Total album length: 1 hour 16 minutes

GOODBYE YELLOW BRICK ROAD

ELTON JOHN

IAN·BECK

17 Off the Wall

| • **Album sales:** 9,850,000 | • **Release date:** August 1979 |

Despite appearing at the end of the decade, *Off the Wall* is one of the seminal albums of the 1970s. Coming off the back of the disco craze, it is also perhaps one of the slickest pop-dance albums ever recorded, thanks in large part to the efforts of producer Quincy Jones, whose partnership with Jackson helped create the wonderfully full disco-funk sound that pervades much of the record.

Although it may not have spawned as many Number One singles—only "Don't Stop 'Til You Get Enough" and "Rock With You" in the US—as his later smash hit album, *Thriller*, it nevertheless marked the point at which Jackson's solo career took an extremely sharp upward curve and the artist became the most recognizable singer on the planet. The album "only" managed to reach Number Three on the US album charts and Number Five in the UK, but it laid the foundations for the creative purple patch that was to carry Jackson through the 1980s.

With songs written by Jackson, Rod Temperton, David Foster, Carole Bayer Sager, and others, *Off the Wall* spawned four Top Ten singles on both sides of the Atlantic, including "Rock With You" and the ballad "She's Out of My Life."

Number One singles:
US: "Don't Stop 'Til You Get Enough"; "Rock With You"

Grammy Awards: None

Label: US & UK: Epic

Recorded in: Los Angeles, USA

Personnel:
Michael Jackson
Louis Johnson
George Duke
John Robinson
Greg Phillinganes
David Williams
Marlo Henderson
Randy Jackson
Richard Heath
Paulinho da Costa
The Seawind Horns

Producer:
Quincy Jones

1. Don't Stop 'Til You Get Enough (6.05)
2. Rock With You (3.40)
3. Workin' Day and Night (5.13)
4. Get on the Floor (4.39)
5. Off the Wall (4.05)
6. Girlfriend (3.04)
7. She's Out of My Life (3.38)
8. I Can't Help It (4.29)
9. It's the Falling in Love (3.48)
10. Burn This Disco Out (3.44)

Total album length: 42 minutes

MICHAEL
JACKSON

OFF
THE
WALL

Sleeve artwork by Mike Salisbury and Steve Harvey

16 Songs in the Key of Life

| • **Album sales:** 10,350,000 | • **Release date:** September 1976 |

Stevie Wonder kept bosses at his label Motown waiting two years for *Songs in the Key of Life*, but their patience was rewarded by the most ambitious project he had yet conceived.

Having recorded six albums of original material in just over three years, Wonder took his time in crafting this wide-ranging set, spread across two discs and an accompanying four-track EP. At this career point, the artist could afford to take his time—six months before the album's release he had signed a seven-year, $13 million deal with his record company, at the time the biggest in recording history.

The album became the first by a US artist to debut at Number One on the Hot 100, while delivering chart-topping singles in "Sir Duke"—Wonder's uplifting tribute to Duke Ellington—and the punchy "I Wish." With 14 weeks in the top slot, the album also combined the gentleness of "Love's In Need of Love Today" with the social awareness of "Black Man" and "Village Ghetto Land." "Isn't She Lovely," which Wonder refused to edit down from its six-and-a-half minutes for single release, honored the birth of his daughter and even contained her early cries.

Number One singles:
US: "Sir Duke"; "I Wish"

Grammy Awards:
Album of the Year; Producer; Best Pop Vocal, Male; Best R&B Vocal Performance: "I Wish"

Label: US: Tamla; UK: Tamla Motown

Recorded in: Los Angeles, New York, & Sausalito, USA

Personnel:
Stevie Wonder
George Benson
Herbie Hancock
Minnie Riperton
Various others

Producer:
Stevie Wonder

1. Love's In Need of Love Today (7:05)
2. Have a Talk With God (2:42)
3. Village Ghetto Land (3:25)
4. Contusion (6:23)
5. Sir Duke (3:45)
6. I Wish (3:54)
7. Knocks Me Off My Feet (4:12)
8. Pastime Paradise (3:36)
9. Summer Soft (3:27)
10. Ordinary Pain (4:14)
11. Isn't She Lovely (6:34)
12. Joy Inside My Tears (6:29)
13. Black Man (8:29)
14. Ngiculela-Es Una Historia-I Am Singalong (3:48)
15. If It's Magic (3:12)
16. As (7:08)
17. Another Star (8:28)
18. Saturn (4:53)
19. Ebony Eyes (4:08)
20. All Day Sucker (5:05)
21. Easy Goin' Evening (My Mama's Call) (3.56)

Album length: 105 minutes

Collector's Album
Includes Two Records
A Something's Extra
Bonus Record
24-Page
Lyric Booklet

Songs In The Key of Life
Stevie Wonder

15 The Stranger

| • **Album sales:** 10,350,000 | • **Release date:** September 1977 |

The Stranger delivered on the promise of earlier albums such as *Streetlife Serenade* and *Turnstiles* to become Billy Joel's breakthrough album. Pairing him for the first time with producer Phil Ramone, the nine-track set offered at times a slicker, more commercial, version of what had come before.

The album's double Grammy-winning ballad "Just the Way You Are" gave Joel his first million-selling, Top 10 single, even though he had to be convinced by Linda Ronstadt and Phoebe

Snow that it was even worthy of inclusion on *The Stranger*. The song has since been covered by more than 200 artists. "Movin' Out" and "She's Always a Woman" also became Top 40 hits, as did "Only the Good Die Young," despite a ban by Catholic radio stations, which deemed it anti-Catholic. "Scenes From an Italian Restaurant," a characteristic Joel observation on New York life, was the result of combining three different songs.

Written entirely by its artist, *The Stranger* went on to become Columbia's all-time second-biggest seller behind Simon and Garfunkel's *Bridge Over Troubled Water*, although it was kept from reaching Number One by the success of the soundtrack to *Saturday Night Fever*.

Number One singles:
None

Grammy Awards:
Record of the Year and Song of the Year: "Just the Way You Are"

Label: US: Columbia; UK: CBS

Recorded in: New York, USA

Producer:
Phil Ramone

Personnel:
Billy Joel
Liberty DeVitto
Ralph McDonald
Richie Cannata
Steve Khan
Dom Cortese
Steve Burgh
Hugh MacDonald
Hugh McCracken
Phil Wood
Doug Stegmeyer
Hiram Bullock
Dave Brown
Richard Tee

1. **Movin' Out (Anthony's Song)** (3:30)
2. **The Stranger** (5:10)
3. **Just the Way You Are** (4:50)
4. **Scenes From an Italian Restaurant** (7:37)
5. **Vienna** (3:34)
6. **Only the Good Die Young** (3:55)
7. **She's Always a Woman** (3:21)
8. **Get It Right the First Time** (3:57)
9. **Everybody Has a Dream** (9:08)

Total album length: 40 minutes

BILLY JOEL   THE STRANGER

Sleeve artwork by Jim Houghton

14 Grease

| • **Album sales:** 10,450,000 | • **Release date:** May 1978 |

Impresario Robert Stigwood was the man with the Midas touch in 1978. He followed up his 1977 movie *Saturday Night Fever*, which had made a star of John Travolta, with an adaptation of the Broadway hit musical *Grease*. The show's transfer to the big screen, with starring roles for Travolta and Olivia Newton-John, took the 1950s-set high school musical to an even higher level of popularity.

The movie added four new songs that became the bedrock of its soundtrack. They included the John Farrar-penned "You're the One That I Want" (at the time the eighth-best-

selling single of all time with in excess of 1.8 million sales), which, alongside the original score's "Summer Nights," became a worldwide duet smash for the movie's two stars. The Bee Gees' Barry Gibb wrote the movie's theme song, which sent Frankie Valli to Number One in the US for the first time in nearly 16 years.

The album was Number One in the US charts for 21 weeks and spent 18 months in the Top 40. In the UK, *Grease* spent 12 weeks at Number One and nearly a year on the charts.

Number One singles:
US & UK: "You're the One That I Want"; US: "Grease"; UK: "Summer Nights"

Grammy Awards: None

Label: RSO

Recorded in:
Los Angeles, USA

Producers:
Louis St Louis
John Farrar
Michael Gibson
Barry Gibb
Karl Richardson

Personnel:
Frankie Valli
John Travolta
Olivia Newton-John
Frankie Avalon
Stockard Channing
Sha-Na-Na

1. Grease (2:37)
2. Summer Nights (3:36)
3. Hopelessly Devoted To You (3:00)
4. You're the One That I Want (2:47)
5. Sandy (2:30)
6. Beauty School Dropout (4:02)
7. Look at Me, I'm Sandra Dee (1:38)
8. Greased Lightnin' (3:12)
9. It's Raining on Prom Night (2:57)
10. Alone at a Drive-in Movie (2:22)
11. Blue Moon (2:18)
12. Rock & Roll is Here To Stay (2:00)
13. Those Magic Changes (2:15)
14. Hound Dog (1:23)
15. Born To Hand Jive (4:39)
16. Tears on My Pillow (2:06)
17. Mooning (2:12)
18. Freddy, My Love (2:40)
19. Rock & Roll Party Queen (2:08)
20. There Are Worse Things I Could Do (2:18)
21. Look at Me, I'm Sandra Dee (1:20)
22. We Go Together (3:14)
23. Love is a Many Spendored Thing (1:23)
24. Grease (reprise) (2:37)

Total album length: 61 minutes

JOHN TRAVOLTA   OLIVIA NEWTON-JOHN

THE ORIGINAL SOUNDTRACK   FROM THE MOTION PICTURE

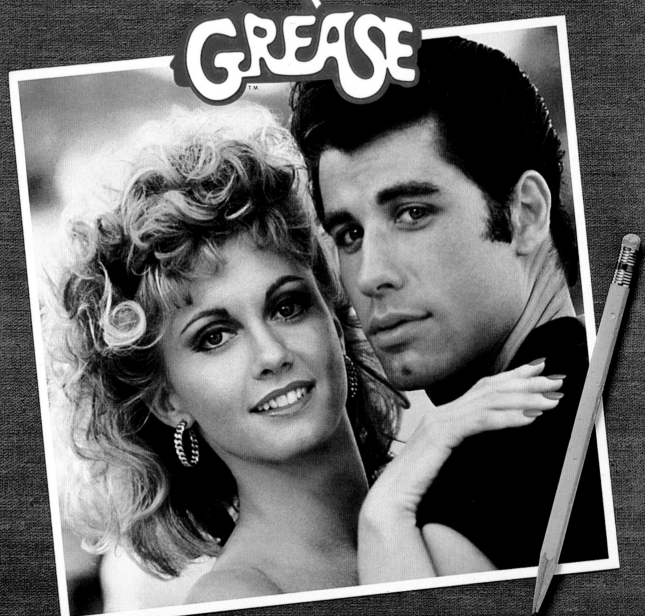

GREASE

13 Van Halen

| • **Album sales:** 10,550,000 | • **Release date:** February 1978 |

Founded by guitarist Eddie van Halen and his drum-playing brother Alex, Van Halen's music is arena in scope but club in attitude. The sound of their debut album was a key element of the band's success; it is upfront and vibrant, and was a big success in the US, certainly for a first record, reaching Number 19 in February 1978. It managed Number 34 in the UK, no less respectable for a newcomer act.

Intriguingly, there is sufficient echo and effects added in the masterful production by Ted Templeman for the whole thing to sound like a live recording. The album featured a new soloing technique called tapping, which used both left and right hands on the guitar neck. During the lead-up to the album's release, Eddie van Halen would play his solos with his back to the audience to hide the technique.

But the production is little without the songs, and tracks such as "Runnin' With the Devil," the guitar frenzy that is "Eruption," and the cover of The Kinks' "You Really Got Me" all illustrate both the dexterity of Eddie's virtuoso guitar playing and David Lee Roth's vocal range. Although it was pure goodtime rock 'n' roll/metal, the band was not averse to mixing things up a bit, as on the eclectic "Ain't Talkin' 'Bout Love."

Number One singles:
None

Grammy Awards: None

Label: US & UK: Warner

Recorded in:
Los Angeles, USA

Personnel:
David Lee Roth
Eddie van Halen
Alex van Halen
Michael Anthony

Producer:
Ted Templeman

1. Runnin' With the Devil (3:32)
2. Atomic Punk (3:30)
3. Eruption (1:42)
4. Feel Your Love Tonight (3:40)
5. You Really Got Me (2:37)
6. Ain't Talkin' 'Bout Love (3:22)
7. Little Dreamer (3:37)
8. Ice Cream Man (3:18)
9. Jamie's Cryin' (3:30)
10. On Fire (3:01)
11. I'm the One (3:44)

Total album length: 35 minutes

VAN HALEN

Van HaleN

12 Tapestry

| • **Album sales:** 11,000,000 | • **Release date:** March 1971 |

With *Tapestry*, Carole King sealed her reputation as not just an outstanding songwriter, but a piano-led singer, too, as well as creating one of the most lastingly popular albums of the 1970s.

Together with her former husband, lyricist Gerry Goffin, King had written a string of hits for others in the previous decade, among them "One Fine Day," "Take Good Care of My Baby," "Up on the Roof," and "The Loco-Motion," but as an artist in her own right *Tapestry* stands as her glorious moment. Two of the album's songs, "Will You Love Me Tomorrow" and "(You Make Me Feel Like) a Natural Woman," are reinterpretations from that period with Goffin, but it is the newer songs, including "So Far Away," "Home Again," and "Beautiful," that notably shine.

The double A-side of "It's Too Late," knowingly charting the breakdown of a relationship, and "I Feel the Earth Move" became a US Number One, reaching Number Six in the UK. "You've Got a Friend" would become a US Number One for James Taylor and is one of King's most covered songs. In turn, Taylor adds backing vocals (as does Joni Mitchell) and guitar to the song's original version on this album.

Tapestry clocked up more than 300 weeks in the US chart, 15 of them at Number One. It was named Album of the Year at the 1971 Grammy Awards.

Number One singles:
US: "It's Too Late/I Feel The Earth Move"

Grammy Awards:
Album of the Year; Best Pop Vocal Performance, Female; Song of the Year: "You've Got a Friend"; Record of the Year: "It's Too Late"

Label: US: Ode; UK: A&M

Recorded in: New York, USA

Personnel:
Carole King
Joel O'Brien
Charles Larkey
Danny Kortchmar
James Taylor
Russ Kunkel
Ralph Schuckett
Joni Mitchell

Producer:
Lou Adler

1. I Feel the Earth Move (2:57)
2. So Far Away (3:56)
3. It's Too Late (3:53)
4. Home Again (2:30)
5. Beautiful (3:06)
6. Way Over Yonder (4:46)
7. You've Got a Friend (5:07)
8. Where You Lead (3:18)
9. Will You Love Me Tomorrow (4:11)
10. Smackwater Jack (3:43)
11. Tapestry (3:12)
12. (You Make Me Feel Like) a Natural Woman (3:39)

Total album length: 45 minutes

Carole King

Carole King Tapestry

Sleeve artwork by Chuck Beeson, Roland Young, and Jim McCrary

11 Bridge Over Troubled Water

| • Album sales: 11,050,000 | • Release date: February 1970 |

Simon and Garfunkel hit their commercial peak, but also the end of the line, with the release of the album *Bridge Over Troubled Water*. The making of what became their final studio album required 800 studio hours, only emphasizing the diverging paths down which the long-time friends were heading.

While the trademark harmonies were evident on the likes of "Cecilia" and "Baby Driver," elsewhere the duo were at loggerheads over song selection. Art Garfunkel rejected Paul Simon's overtly political "Cuba Si, Nixon No," while Simon turned away his colleague's Bach chorale-like track. Even the gospel-styled title track created tensions. Garfunkel persuaded Simon to write a third verse to the song, much to the songwriter's chagrin, and initially insisted that Simon should sing the number himself. Garfunkel's eventual angelic delivery turned it into a landmark recording, although it angered Simon when Garfunkel won all the concert applause for what was his song.

Bridge Over Troubled Water spent 10 weeks as the US Number One, while in the UK its 41-week chart-topping run remains the longest for a pop-rock release. Collectively, as an album and single, *Bridge Over Troubled Water* won an unprecedented six Grammy Awards.

Number One singles:
US & UK: "Bridge Over Troubled Water"

Grammy Awards:
Album of the Year; Best Engineered Record; Best Arrangement Accompanying Vocalists; Record of the Year, Song of the Year and Best Contemporary Song: "Bridge Over Troubled Water"

Label: US: CBS;
UK: Columbia

Recorded in: New York & Los Angeles, USA

Personnel:
Paul Simon
Art Garfunkel
Hal Blaine
Larry Knechtel
Fred Carter
Pete Drake

Producers:
Simon and Garfunkel
Roy Halee

1. Bridge Over Troubled Water (4:55)
2. El Condor Pasa (If I Could) (3:09)
3. Cecilia (2:54)
4. Keep the Customer Satisfied (2:37)
5. So Long, Frank Lloyd Wright (3:45)
6. The Boxer (5:12)
7. Baby Driver (3:17)
8. The Only Living Boy in New York (4:01)
9. Why Don't You Write Me (2:46)
10. Bye Bye Love (2:52)
11. Song For the Asking (1:59)

Total album length: 36 minutes

63699

CBS

Stereo
Can also be
played on mono
equipment
See note over

Simon
and
Garfunkel
Bridge
Over
Troubled
Water

Sleeve artwork by Tony Lane

10 Houses of the Holy

| • **Album sales:** 11,500,000 | • **Release date:** March 1973 |

Ever the ones to surprise both fans and critics, Led Zeppelin revealed a new side to their musical creativity with *Houses of the Holy*. Not only does the album show the band's sense of humor, with offbeat tracks such as the James Brown tribute "The Crunge," it also mixes up the styles along the way. There's "cod" reggae with "D'Yer Mak'er," the ballad-like subtlety of "The Rain Song," alongside a hard and fast rocking track such as "The Ocean." Only on songs such as "Over the Hills and Far Away" and "Dancing Days" does the band sound anything like the Zeppelin people had come to know.

Attempts to straddle influences, past and present, did not prevent the album's commercial success. The record found favor, as usual, in the US, where it reached the top of the Hot 100, while it also went to Number One in the UK. "Over the Hills and Far Away" and "D'Yer Mak'er" both made the Top 20, and Led Zeppelin's US tour in the summer of 1973 broke the box office records set by The Beatles. On the first two days of the tour alone, more than 100,000 fans saw the band in concert.

The title *Houses of the Holy* is a dedication by the band to their fans who appeared at their venues dubbed "houses of the holy." The track "The Ocean" is also dedicated to the "sea" of fans who attended Led Zeppelin concerts.

Number One singles:
None

Grammy Awards: None

Label: US & UK: Atlantic

Recorded in: London, UK

Personnel:
Robert Plant
Jimmy Page
John Bonham
John Paul Jones

Producers:
Jimmy Page
Peter Grant

1. **The Song Remains the Same** (5:30)
2. **The Rain Song** (7:38)
3. **Over the Hills and Far Away** (4:50)
4. **The Crunge** (3:17)
5. **Dancing Days** (3:43)
6. **D'Yer Mak'er** (4:22)
7. **No Quarter** (7:00)
8. **The Ocean** (4:31)

Total album length: 41 minutes

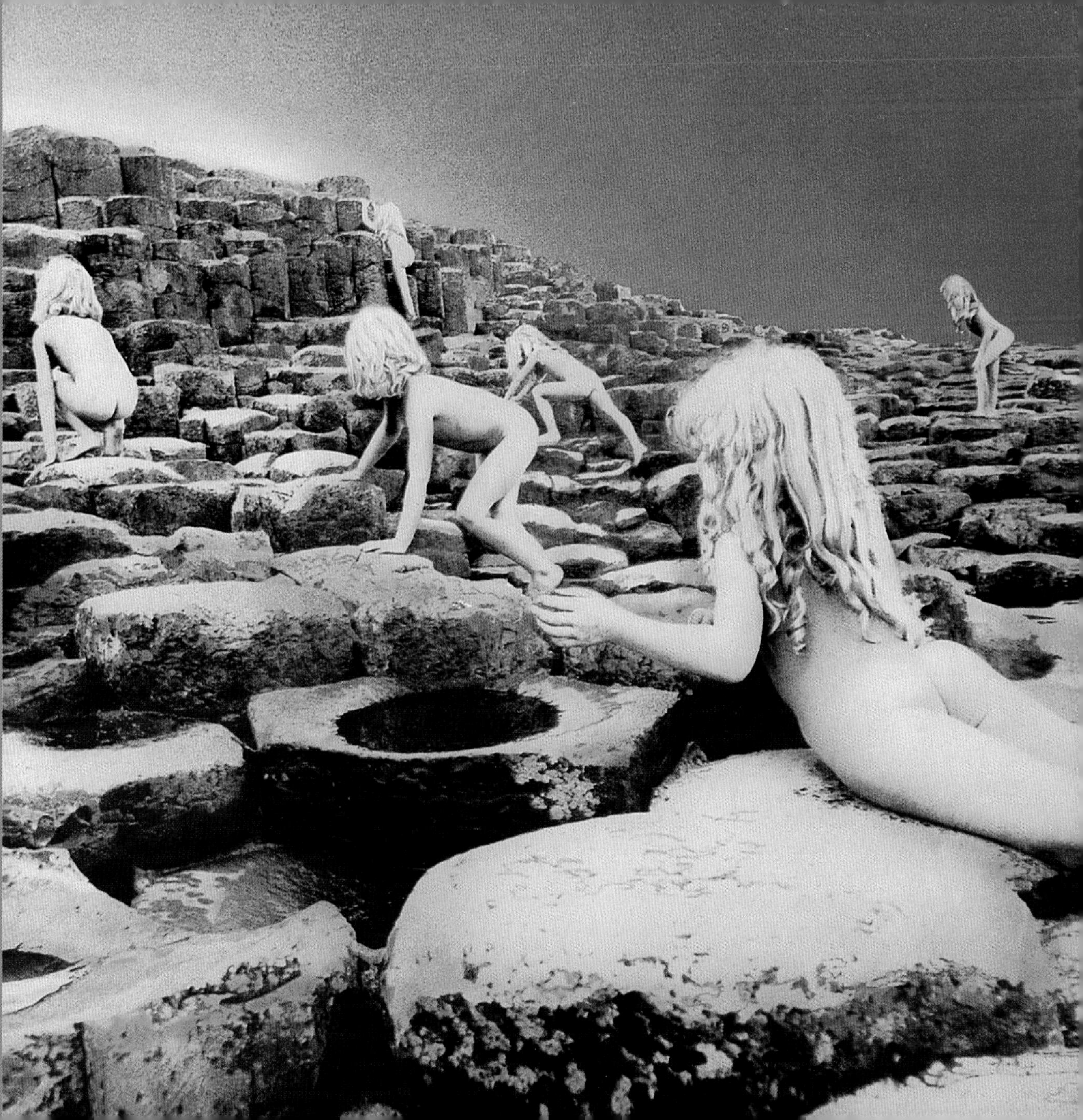

Sleeve artwork by Hipgnosis

9 Physical Graffiti

| • **Album sales:** 16,650,000 | • **Release date:** February 1975 |

Arriving nearly two years after its predecessor, *Physical Graffiti* was the final confirmation—if confirmation were needed—that Led Zeppelin were more than just any old supergroup. The album topped the US and UK album charts, and shortly after its release the entire Led Zeppelin catalog of six albums was simultaneously on the top 200 album chart—a feat never before accomplished.

Physical Graffiti was Zeppelin's first double album and their first release on Swan Song, the record label established by the band in 1974. A number of tracks, notably "Kashmir" and "In My Time of Dying"—redolent of the lengthy blues songs that they had recorded in their early career—became live favorites, and featured in

a series of dates at London's 21,000-capacity Earl's Court arena, the biggest gigs the band had played in the UK up to that date.

Elsewhere on the album they even managed to pump funky vibes into the rock composition "Trampled Under Foot." There was still room for a lighter touch, and the second record features some classic if unlikely Zeppelin songs, including the bar-room boogie "Boogie With Stu," the acoustic instrumental "Bron-Y-Aur," and the hauntingly melodic "Ten Years Gone."

Number One singles:
None

Grammy Awards: None

Label: US & UK: Swan Song

Recorded in: Various locations, UK

Personnel:
Robert Plant
Jimmy Page
John Bonham
John Paul Jones

Producers:
Jimmy Page
Peter Grant

1. Custard Pie (4:13)
2. The Rover (5:37)
3. In My Time of Dying (11:06)
4. Houses of the Holy (4:02)
5. Trampled Under Foot (5:36)
6. Kashmir (8:28)
7. In the Light (8:46)
8. Bron-Y-Aur (2:06)
9. Down By the Seaside (5:16)
10. Ten Years Gone (6:33)
11. Night Flight (3:37)
12. The Wanton Song (4:09)
13. Boogie With Stu (3:53)
14. Black Country Woman (4:32)
15. Sick Again (4:43)

Total album length: 82 minutes

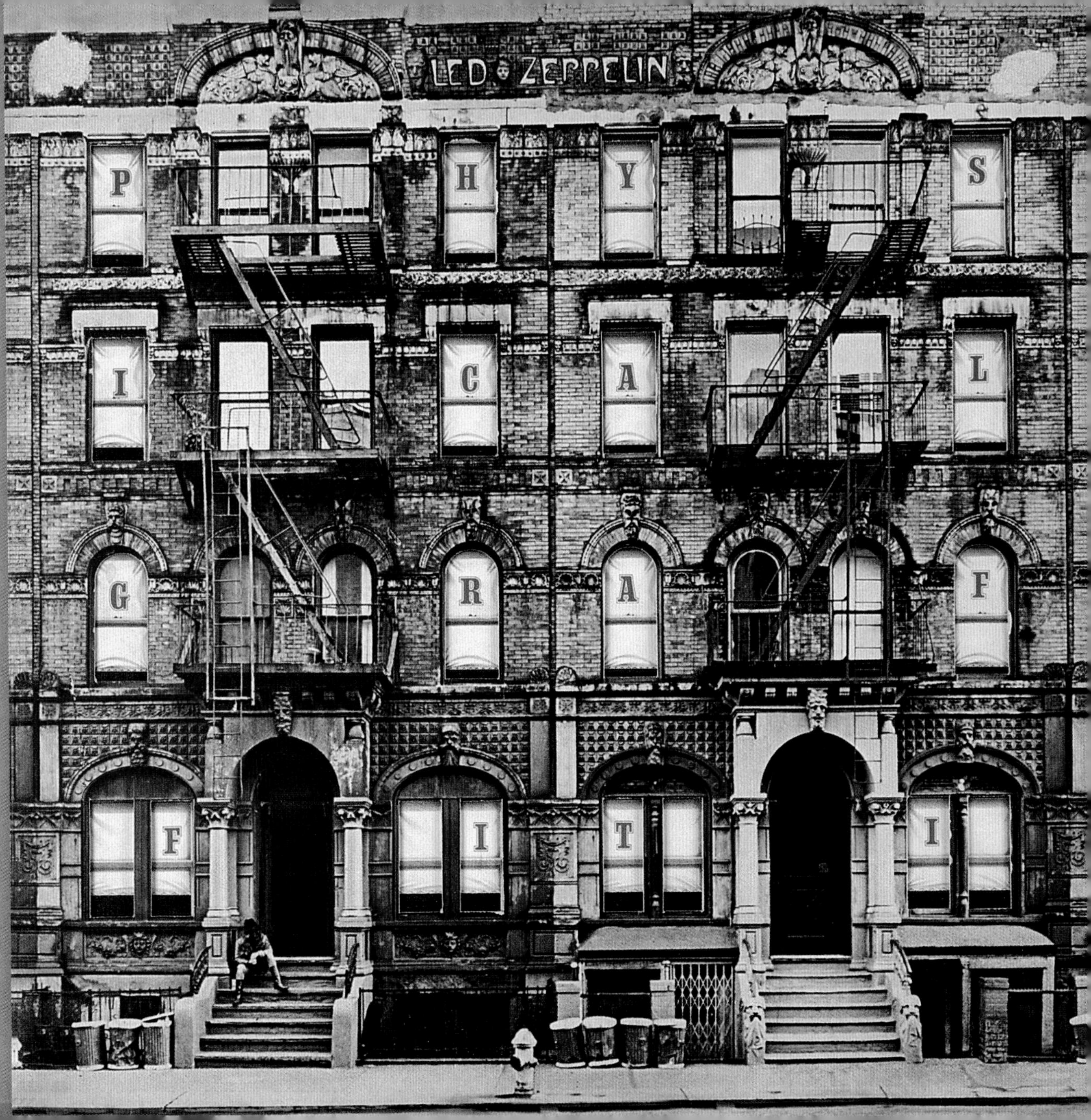

Sleeve artwork by Peter Corriston and Mike Doud

8 Bat Out of Hell

| • **Album sales:** 17,050,000 | • **Release date:** October 1977 |

Meat Loaf's powerful, uncompromising voice and Jim Steinman's Wagnerian rock epics created the perfect storm to turn *Bat Out of Hell* into one of the biggest-selling debut albums of all time. Emerging from a Steinman musical set in the future around the story of Peter Pan, the album is practically in a category all by itself, scaling almost operatic heights on the likes of the near 10-minute title track and "Paradise By the Dashboard Light."

Such was the ambition of the project that it took four years from its inception to finally earn a release, having been rejected along the way by several record executives before winning finance from a label owned by musician Todd Rundgren, who ended up producing the album. Rundgren, who plays guitar on the record, is the vital third ingredient, providing the ideal setting for Steinman's overblown ideas and Meat Loaf's dramatic delivery.

Even after finally winning a release on October 21, 1977, *Bat Out of Hell* took another six months to crack the US Top 40, peaking at 14 in an 82-week chart run as the extracted "Two Out of Three Ain't Bad" became a million-seller in its own right. The album's UK chart performance was even more remarkable, setting an all-time run of 471 weeks.

Number One singles:
None

Grammy Awards: None

Label: US & UK: Epic/Cleveland International

Recorded in: New York, USA

Producer:
Todd Rundgren

Personnel:
Meat Loaf
Todd Rundgren
Kasim Sulton
Max Weinberg
John Wilcox
Jim Steinman
Roy Bittan
Cheryl Hardwick
Steven Margoshes
Roger Powell
Jimmy Iovine
John Jansen
Ed Sprague
Mark Thomas
Edgar Winter

1. **Bat Out of Hell** (9:51)
2. **You Took the Words Right Out of My Mouth (Hot Summer Night)** (5:04)
3. **Heaven Can Wait** (4:41)
4. **All Revved Up With No Place To Go** (4:20)
5. **Two Out of Three Ain't Bad** (5:25)
6. **Paradise By the Dashboard Light** (8:28)
7. **For Crying Out Loud** (8:44)

Total album length: 46 minutes

Meat Loaf
BAT OUT OF HELL

Sleeve artwork by Ed Lee and Richard Corben

SONGS BY JIM STEINMAN

7 Saturday Night Fever

| • **Album sales:** 17,150,000 | • **Release date:** November 1977 |

Just a few years before *Saturday Night Fever*, the Bee Gees' music had so fallen out of favor that their record company refused to release one of their albums. In contrast, the soundtrack to the movie *Saturday Night Fever*, on which the Bee Gees led the songwriting both for themselves and other artists, dominated the US album chart for the first half of 1978, with 24 weeks at Number One; it also reached Number One in the UK.

The album that still defines the sound of disco spawned three US Number Ones for the Bee Gees ("Night Fever," "How Deep Is Your Love," and "Stayin' Alive") and a Number One for Yvonne Elliman with the Bee Gees-penned "If I Can't Have You." It also included the Bee Gees' previous chart-toppers "Jive Talkin'" and "You Should Be Dancing."

Number One singles:
US: "Stayin' Alive"; "How Deep Is Your Love"; "If I Can't Have You";
US & UK: "Night Fever"

Grammy Awards:
Album of the Year; Producer of the Year; Best Pop Vocal Performance by a Group: "How Deep Is Your Love" and "Stayin' Alive"; Best Arrangement for Voices: "Stayin' Alive"

Label: US: RSO;
UK: Polydor

Recorded in: Paris, France

Personnel:
Robin Gibb
Maurice Gibb
Barry Gibb
Yvonne Elliman
Walter Murphy
David Shire
Ralph MacDonald
Kool & The Gang
KC & The Sunshine Band
MFSB
Tavares
The Trammps

Producers:
The Bee Gees
Karl Richardson
Albhy Galuten
Various others

1. **Stayin' Alive**
   (The Bee Gees) (4:45)
2. **How Deep Is Your Love**
   (The Bee Gees) (4:05)
3. **Night Fever**
   (The Bee Gees) (3:33)
4. **More Than a Woman**
   (The Bee Gees) (3:17)
5. **If I Can't Have You**
   (Yvonne Elliman) (3:00)
6. **A Fifth of Beethoven**
   (Walter Murphy) (3:03)
7. **More Than a Woman**
   (Tavares) (3:17)
8. **Manhattan Skyline**
   (David Shire) (4:44)
9. **Calypso Breakdown**
   (Ralph MacDonald)
   (7:50)
10. **Night on the Disco Mountain**
    (David Shire) (05:12)
11. **Open Sesame**
    (Kool & The Gang) (4:01)
12. **Jive Talkin'**
    (The Bee Gees) (3:43)
13. **You Should Be Dancing**
    (The Bee Gees) (4:14)
14. **Boogie Shoes**
    (KC & The Sunshine Band) (2:17)
15. **Salsation**
    (David Shire) (3:50)
16. **K-Jee** (MFSB) (4:13)
17. **Disco Inferno**
    (The Trammps) (10:51)

Total album length: 76 minutes

THE ORIGINAL MOVIE SOUND TRACK

Saturday Night Fever

6 Boston

• Album sales: 17,600,000 | • Release date: June 1977

Boston was one of the few "corporate rock" albums to contain the germ of something more than the usual bland, edgeless music produced by the group's peers.

The brainchild of Tom Scholz, who recorded countless demos in a home-built basement studio, including six that led to eight tracks on the album, Boston's eponymous debut captured millions of US and UK radio listeners with a blend of melodic, well-crafted AOR, spine-tingling harmonies and intelligent instrumentation. It soon became the largest-selling debut album of all time and the best-selling debut album by a group. The band quickly went from being virtually unknown to playing sold-out arena shows all over the US.

The record's opening track, "More Than a Feeling," was an immediate success on US radio and in the UK, reaching Numbers Five and 22 respectively. There are thoughtful songs in here, too, notably "Hitch a Ride" and the album's closer, "Let Me Take You Home Tonight."

Brad Delp's incredibly sopranic vocals and Tom Scholz's fantastic guitar work are both Boston trademarks. This album showcases both of those talents admirably.

Creem magazine voted the album's cover one of the Top Ten Album Covers of the Year in 1977.

Number One singles:
None

Grammy Awards: None

Label: US & UK: Epic

Recorded in: Los Angeles, USA

Personnel:
Tom Scholz
Brad Delp
Barry Goudreau
Fran Sheehan
Sib Hashian

Producers:
John Boylan
Tom Scholz

1. **More Than a Feeling** (4:45)
2. **Peace of Mind** (5:03)
3. **Foreplay Long Time** (7:51)
4. **Rock & Roll Band** (3:00)
5. **Smokin** (4:21)
6. **Hitch a Ride** (4:11)
7. **Something About You** (3:48)
8. **Let Me Take You Home Tonight** (4:45)

Total album length: 38 minutes

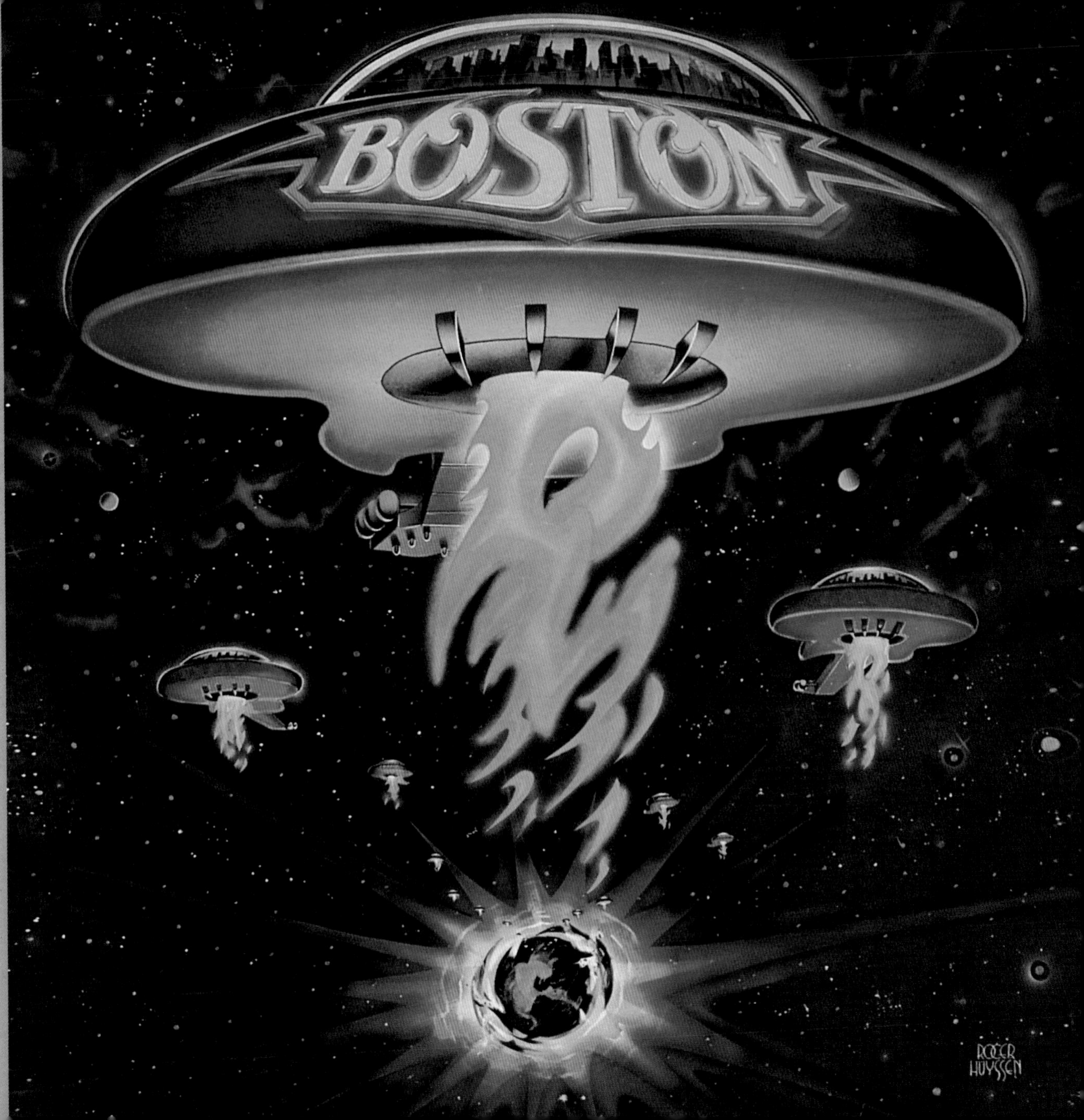

BOSTON

ROGER HUYSSEN

5 Hotel California

| • **Album sales:** 17,850,000 | • **Release date:** December 1976 |

The Eagles moved still further from their early country roots and cranked up the guitars to produce their most rock-flavored material yet on *Hotel California*. With the addition of guitarist Joe Walsh to the lineup as a replacement for the more country-leaning Bernie Leadon, the band turned out a harder-edged sound for what represents the creative and commercial peak of their incredibly successful career.

Standing, too, as a definitive statement on 1970s American rock, *Hotel California* was the result of six months' work, not recorded in California, but Miami's Criteria Studios. Expectations only swelled ahead of its release by a gap of almost a year and a half since their last studio effort, *One of These Nights*.

The new album provided a metaphor for the excesses of aspects of American society and, in particular, Californian life, not least on the epic six-and-a-half-minute title track, made all the more distinctive by duo guitar solos from Walsh and the song's cowriter Don Felder. The track, one of five numbers here sung by drummer Don Henley, gave the band a fourth Hot 100 number one just 10 weeks after fellow album cut "New Kid in Town" had reached the top.

Spread across four separate runs, the album accumulated eight weeks at Number One in the US in early 1977, while it achieved a Number Two spot in the UK.

Number One singles:
US: "Hotel California";
"New Kid in Town"

Grammy Awards:
Record of the Year:
"Hotel California"; Best
Arrangement for Voices:
"New Kid in Town"

Label:
US & UK: Asylum

Recorded in: Miami, USA

Personnel:
Don Henley
Glenn Frey
Don Felder
Randy Meisner
Joe Walsh

Producer:
Bill Szymczyk

1. **Hotel California** (6:30)
2. **New Kid in Town** (5:04)
3. **Life in the Fast Lane** (4:46)
4. **Wasted Time** (4:55)
5. **Wasted Time (reprise)** (1:22)
6. **Victim of Love** (4:11)
7. **Pretty Maids All in a Row** (4:05)
8. **Try and Love Again** (5:10)
9. **The Last Resort** (7:25)

Total album length: 43 minutes

Hotel California

4 Dark Side of the Moon

| • **Album sales:** 19,250,000 | • **Release date:** March 1973 |

Pink Floyd's eighth album, recorded at London's Abbey Road Studios, took more than eight months to produce—an extremely long time for its day. The album was launched at a special listening session at London's Planetarium in January 1973. *Dark Side of the Moon* topped the US album chart, where it stayed for more than 300 weeks. In the UK, the album reached Number Two and has continued to sell well ever since.

The album's first single, "Money"—which includes a rhythmic accompaniment created from the sampled sounds of clinking coins and cash registers—reached Number 13 on the US Hot 100, although it failed to make a great impression on the UK charts. To make the sampled money sounds fit the 7/4 beat, the tape had to be cut up and stuck back together, using a ruler to make sure the beats were accurate. A second single from the album, "Us and Them," was released in October 1973, but failed to make it into the top 100 in either the UK or the US.

A number of voices were used on the *Dark Side of the Moon*, including the band's tour manager and roadie. Paul McCartney's voice was recorded but not actually used.

Number One singles:
None

Grammy Awards:
Best Engineered Album

Label: Harvest

Recorded in: London, UK

Producers:
Pink Floyd

Personnel:
Dave Gilmour
Roger Waters
Rick Wright
Nick Mason
Barry St John
Dick Parry
Doris Troy
Claire Torry
Liza Stuke
Lesley Duncan

1. Speak To Me (1:08)
2. Breathe in the Air (2:48)
3. On the Run (3:50)
4. Time (6:49)
5. The Great Gig In the Sky (4:44)
6. Money (6:22)
7. Us and Them (7:49)
8. Any Colour You Like (3:26)
9. Brain Damage (3:46)
10. Eclipse (2:11)

Total album length: 43 minutes

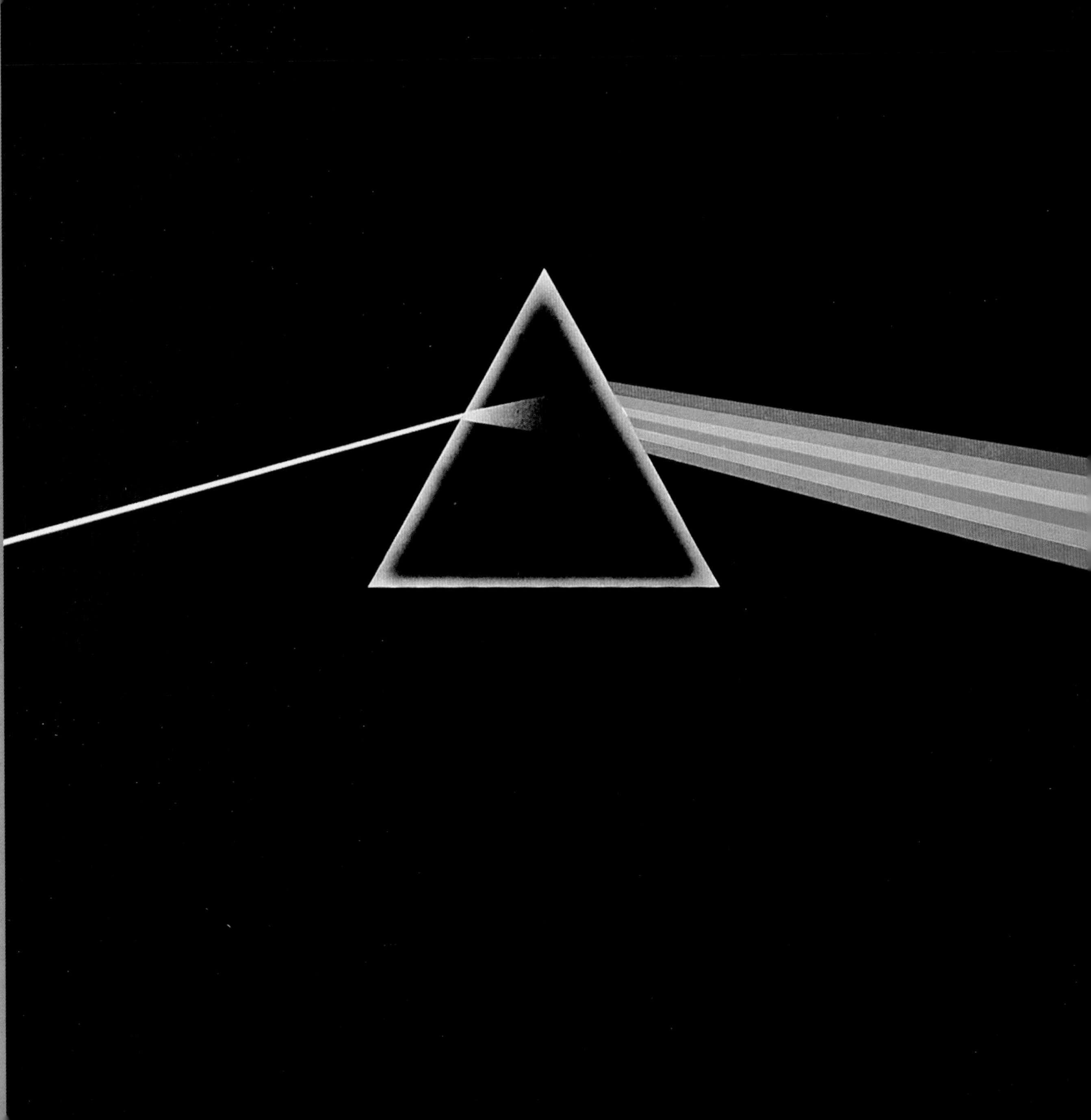

Sleeve artwork by George Hardie of NTA and Hipgnosis

3 Rumours

• **Album sales:** 23,350,000 | • **Release date:** February 1977

*R*umours is Fleetwood Mac's 11th album and its biggest-selling one. A Number One album on both sides of the Atlantic, *Rumours* debuted at Number 10 and went on to spend 31 weeks at Number One in the US and almost a year in the Top Five, the longest stint in the 1970s. The record produced no fewer than four hit singles for the band: "Go Your Own Way," "Don't Stop," "You Make Loving Fun," and the US Number One "Dreams" (which reached Number 24 in the UK). The record spent 450 weeks in the UK listings.

The group's second album with its most famous lineup—Fleetwood, Buckingham and his then-girlfriend, singer Stevie Nicks, John McVie, and his ex-wife, singer and keyboardist Christine McVie—*Rumours* tracks the twin couples as they split. The record features Nicks at her huskiest, and contains bittersweet love songs such as "Go Your Own Way" and "I Don't Wanna Know."

The songwriting duties were once more shared among the band, with Buckingham and Nicks pitching in on songs such as "Go Your Own Way" and "Dreams," and Christine McVie penning the achingly beautiful "Songbird," among others. *Rumours* was chosen as the 25th greatest album of all time by the editors of *Rolling Stone* magazine in December 2003.

Number One singles:
US: "Dreams"

Grammy Awards:
Album of the Year

Label: US & UK: Warner

Recorded in: Los Angeles, USA

Personnel:
Lindsey Buckingham
Stevie Nicks
John McVie
Christine McVie
Mick Fleetwood

Producers:
Fleetwood Mac
Richard Dashut
Ken Caillat

1. Second Hand News (2:46)
2. Dreams (4:17)
3. Never Going Back Again (2:14)
4. Don't Stop (3:12)
5. Go Your Own Way (3:39)
6. Songbird (3:21)
7. The Chain (4:30)
8. You Make Loving Fun (3:36)
9. I Don't Wanna Know (3:16)
10. Oh Daddy (3:53)
11. Gold Dust Woman (4:53)

Total album length: 39 minutes

2 The Wall

| • **Album sales:** 24,300,000 | • **Release date:** December 1979 |

The subject matter of Pink Floyd's 11th album may be bleak—the mental decline of a rock star—but a heavier focus on songs rather than experimental soundscaping gave *The Wall* increased appeal. It made Number One in the US—where it remained for 15 weeks—and Number Three in the UK.

For a band not previously noted for their singles, "Another Brick in the Wall, Part 2" broke with tradition, topping the charts in both the US and UK, as well as reaching the Top Five in 19 other countries. Another highlight is "Comfortably Numb," a collaboration between guitarist David Gilmour and bassist Roger Waters.

Waters based *The Wall* on his own experiences of fame, and found little creative space for drummer Nick Mason or keyboardist Rick Wright.

The album's success was consolidated with a movie version in 1982, featuring animation from Gerald Scarfe.

Number One singles:
US & UK: "Another Brick in the Wall, Part 2"

Grammy Awards:
None

Label: US: Tower;
UK: Columbia

Recorded in:
Miravel, France; Los Angeles, USA; New York, USA

Personnel:
David Gilmour
Richard Wright
Roger Waters
Nick Mason
Bruce Johnston
Toni Tenille
Joe Chemay
John Joyce
Stan Farber
Jim Haas

Producers:
Bob Ezrin
David Gilmour
Roger Waters

1. In the Flesh (3:19)
2. The Thin Ice (2:29)
3. Another Brick in the Wall, Part 1 (3:09)
4. The Happiest Days of Our Lives (1:51)
5. Another Brick in the Wall, Part 2 (3:59)
6. Mother (5:36)
7. Goodbye Blue Sky (2:48)
8. Empty Spaces (2:08)
9. Young Lust (3:30)
10. One of My Turns (3:37)
11. Don't Leave Me Now (4:17)
12. Another Brick in the Wall, Part 3 (1:14)
13. Goodbye Cruel World (1:17)
14. Hey You (4:42)
15. Is There Anybody Out There? (2:40)
16. Nobody Home (3:24)
17. Vera (1:33)
18. Bring the Boys Back Home (1:27)
19. Comfortably Numb (6:24)
20. The Show Must Go On (1:35)
21. In the Flesh (4:17)
22. Run Like Hell (4:24)
23. Waiting For the Worms (3:58)
24. Stop (0:30)
25. The Trial (5:20)
26. Outside the Wall (1:44)

Total album length: 81:12

1

Led Zeppelin IV (Four Symbols)

| • **Album sales:** 24,850,000 | • **Release date:** November 1971 |

By the time Led Zeppelin recorded "*IV*"—the album is officially untitled—the band was well on the way to becoming the biggest rock 'n' roll outfit in the world.

From the opening riff that launches into "Black Dog" and then refuses to let up with the album's second track, "Rock and Roll," the record is a testament to rock music in the early 1970s. But Zeppelin also paid heed to their folk-blues roots, with the Tolkienesque "The Battle For Evermore," featuring English folk diva and Fairport Convention vocalist Sandy Denny, and "Going To California."

The album is today perhaps best known for featuring the eight-minute, three-part "Stairway To Heaven," one of the few songs of its type to be able to live up to the label "epic." The track is the most requested song on US rock 'n' roll radio history and now regarded as one of the greatest rock songs of all time. It is also the biggest-selling single piece of sheet music in rock history. Many fans regard the album's closing track, "When the Levee Breaks," as equally powerful.

"*IV*" topped the album chart in the UK and reached the Number Two spot in the US. In terms of singles, the opening track "Black Dog" only reached Number 15 in the US charts, while second single "Rock and Roll," featuring The Rolling Stones' regular pianist Ian Stewart, failed to break into the Top 40.

Despite pressure from Atlantic Records, the band refused to edit down "Stairway To Heaven" to release it as a single.

Number One singles:
None

Grammy Awards: None

Label: US & UK: Atlantic

Recorded in:
Hampshire & London, UK;
Los Angeles, USA

Personnel:
Robert Plant
Jimmy Page
John Paul Jones
John Bonham
Sandy Denny
Ian Stewart

Producers:
Jimmy Page
Peter Grant

1. **Black Dog** (4:54)
2. **Rock and Roll** (3:40)
3. **The Battle For Evermore** (5:51)
4. **Stairway To Heaven** (8:00)
5. **Misty Mountain Hop** (4:38)
6. **Four Sticks** (4:44)
7. **Going To California** (3:31)
8. **When the Levee Breaks** (7:07)

Total album length: 42 minutes

Sleeve artwork by Graphreaks and Barrington Coleby

Appendix: Facts and figures

The 20 highest-ranking US artists (position on list given in brackets)

1 Fleetwood Mac (US/UK): *Rumours* (3)
2 The Eagles: *Hotel California* (5)
3 Boston: *Boston* (6)
4 Meat Loaf: *Bat Out of Hell* (8)
5 Simon & Garfunkel: *Bridge Over Troubled Water* (11)
6 Carole King: *Tapestry* (12)
7 Van Halen: *Van Halen* (13)
8 Billy Joel: *The Stranger* (15)
9 Stevie Wonder: *Songs in the Key of Life* (16)
10 Michael Jackson: *Off the Wall* (17)
11 Aerosmith: *Toys in the Attic* (19)
12 Crosby, Stills, Nash & Young (US/Canada/UK): *Déjà Vu* (22)
13 Jackson Browne: *Running on Empty* (23)
14 Foreigner (US/UK): *Double Vision* (28)
15 Bruce Springsteen: *Born To Run* (30)
16 The Cars: *The Cars* (35)
17 Bob Seger & the Silver Bullet Band: *Night Moves* (36)
18 Willy Nelson: *Stardust* (39)
19 Elvis Presley: *Aloha From Hawaii* (42)
20 Santana: *Abraxas* (43)

The 20 highest-ranking UK or international artists

1 Led Zeppelin: *Led Zeppelin IV* (1)
2 Pink Floyd: *The Wall* (2)
3 Fleetwood Mac (US/UK): *Rumours* (3)
4 Elton John: *Goodbye Yellow Brick Road* (18)
5 Peter Frampton: *Frampton Comes Alive!* (20)
6 AC/DC (Australia): *Highway To Hell* (21)
7 Crosby, Stills, Nash & Young (US/Canada/UK): *Déjà Vu* (22)
8 Foreigner (US/UK): *Double Vision* (28)
9 George Harrison: *All Things Must Pass* (33)
10 The Rolling Stones: *Some Girls* (34)
11 Bad Company: *Bad Company* (41)
12 Neil Young: *Harvest* (48)
13 The Beatles: *Let It Be* (50)
14 Black Sabbath: *Paranoid* (51)
15 Supertramp: *Breakfast in America* (53)
16 Queen: *News of the World* (56)
17 Rod Stewart: *Blondes Have More Fun* (63)
18 The Who: *Who's Next* (64)
19 McCartney And Wings: *Band on the Run* (69)
20 Jethro Tull: *Aqualung* (71)

The 10 highest-ranking solo artists

1 Meat Loaf: *Bat Out of Hell* (8)
2 Carole King: *Tapestry* (12)
3 Billy Joel: *The Stranger* (15)
4 Stevie Wonder: *Songs in the Key of Life* (16)
5 Michael Jackson: *Off the Wall* (17)
6 Elton John: *Goodbye Yellow Brick Road* (18)
7 Peter Frampton: *Frampton Comes Alive!* (20)
8 Jackson Browne: *Running on Empty* (23)
9 Bruce Springsteen: *Born To Run* (30)
10 George Harrison: *All Things Must Pass* (33)

The 10 highest-ranking bands

1 Led Zeppelin: *Led Zeppelin IV* (1)
2 Pink Floyd: *The Wall* (2)
3 Fleetwood Mac: *Rumours* (3)
4 The Eagles: *Hotel California* (5)
5 Boston: *Boston* (6)
6 Simon & Garfunkel: *Bridge Over Troubled Water* (11)
7 Van Halen: *Van Halen* (13)
8 Aerosmith: *Toys in the Attic* (19)
9 AC/DC: *Highway To Hell* (21)
10 Crosby, Stills, Nash & Young: *Déjà Vu* (22)

Record labels with the most albums in the Top 100

1 Columbia (22 albums)
2 CBS (16 albums)
3 Atlantic (10 albums)
4 A&M (8 albums)
5 Warner Brothers (7 albums)
6 Asylum (5 albums)
7 Capitol (5 albums)
8 Elektra (5 albums)
9 Reprise (5 albums)
10 Swan Song (5 albums)
11 Epic (4 albums)
12 Island (4 albums)
13 MCA (4 albums)
14 RCA Victor (3 albums)
15 Apple (3 albums)
16 DJM (3 albums)
17 Harvest (3 albums)
18 Rolling Stones (3 albums)
19 RSO (3 albums)
20 EMI (3 albums)

Artists with three or more albums in the Top 100
(artists ranked by number of albums and aggregate score of album positions)

1 **Led Zeppelin:**
Led Zeppelin IV (1)
Physical Graffiti (9)
Houses of the Holy (10)
Led Zeppelin III (31)
In Through the Out Door (32)
The Song Remains the Same (52)
Presence (68)

2 **Pink Floyd:**
The Wall (2)
Dark Side of the Moon (4)
Wish You Were Here (27)
Animals (49)

3 **The Eagles:**
Hotel California (5)
The Long Run (24)
One of These Nights (55)

4 **Foreigner:**
Double Vision (28)
Foreigner (45)
Head Games (46)

5 **Bob Seger & The Silver Bullet Band:**
Night Moves (36)
Stranger in Town (37)
Live Bullet (38)

6 **Elton John:**
Goodbye Yellow Brick Road (18)
Captain Fantastic and the Brown Dirt Cowboy (75)
Don't Shoot Me I'm Only the Piano Player (88)

7 **The Rolling Stones:**
Some Girls (34)
Sticky Fingers (66)
Goat's Head Soup (77)

8 **Earth, Wind & Fire:**
All 'N All (81)
Gratitude (85)
That's the Way of the World (86)

Albums containing the most Number One singles

1 *Saturday Night Fever*: **Original Soundtrack**
4 Number Ones: US: "Stayin' Alive"; "How Deep Is Your Love"; "If I Can't Have You"; US & UK: "Night Fever"

2 *Grease:* **Original Soundtrack**
3 Number Ones: US & UK: "You're the One That I Want"; US: "Grease"; UK: "Summer Nights"

3 *Let It Be*: **The Beatles**
3 Number Ones: US & UK: "Get Back"; US: "Let It Be"; "The Long and Winding Road"

4 *Hotel California*: **The Eagles**
2 Number Ones: US: "Hotel California"; "New Kid in Town"

5 *Tapestry*: **Carole King**
2 Number Ones: US: "It's Too Late"; "You've Got a Friend"

6 *Songs in the Key of Life*: **Stevie Wonder**
2 Number Ones: US: "Sir Duke"; "I Wish"

7 *Off the Wall*: **Michael Jackson**
2 Number Ones: US: "Don't Stop 'Til You Get Enough"; "Rock With You"

Albums that have won the most Grammys

1 *Bridge Over Troubled Water*: Simon & Garfunkel (6 Grammys)
2 *Saturday Night Fever*: Soundtrack (4)
3 *Tapestry*: Carole King (4)
4 *Songs in the Key of Life*: Stevie Wonder (4)
5 *Minute By Minute*: The Doobie Brothers (4)
6 *Hotel California*: The Eagles (2)
7 *The Stranger*: Billy Joel (2)
8 *52nd Street*: Billy Joel (2)
9 *A Star Is Born*: Streisand/Kristofferson (2)
10 *All 'N All*: Earth, Wind & Fire (2)

The 5 highest-ranking soundtracks

1 *Saturday Night Fever*, Various Artists (7)
2 *Grease*, Various Artists (14)
3 *A Star Is Born,* Streisand/Kristofferson (54)
4 *The Song Remains the Same*, Led Zeppelin (52)
5 *That's the Way of the World*, Earth, Wind & Fire (86)

The 5 highest-ranking live albums

1 *Frampton Comes Alive!*, Peter Frampton (20)
2 *"Live" Bullet*, Bob Seger & The Silver Bullet Band (38)
3 *Aloha From Hawaii*, Elvis Presley (42)
4 *The Song Remains the Same*, Led Zeppelin (52)
5 *One More From the Road*, Lynyrd Skynyrd (74)

Index

Index

Acknowledgments

Thanks to HMV (hmv.co.uk) for their help in researching and supplying the albums featured in this book
Thanks to the following for help with supplying the albums as well as for their invaluable industry knowledge: Reckless Records (www.reckless.co.uk), Islington, London; Flashback (www.flashback.co.uk), Islington, London; Golden Grooves (www.goldengroovesrecords.com), Old Street, London; Haggle (www.hagglevinyl.com), Islington, London; The Music and Video Exchange, Notting Hill, London; Stage and Screen, Notting Hill, London; Beanos (www.beanos.co.uk)
©Apple Corps Ltd: The Beatles, page 116, ©Promotone BV: The Rolling Stones, page 149, ©Virgin: The Rolling Stones, pages 63, 85

Author: Hamish Champ, an experienced music journalist, has written about the music and entertainment industries for a wide range of publications, including *Billboard* and *Music & Media,* and has also edited *Music Business International* magazine.

Picture Credits: FRONT COVER: (top) Original Soundtrack: *Saturday Night Fever*, Eagles: *Hotel California*, Led Zeppelin: *Led Zeppelin III* (bottom) Bruce Springsteen: *Born To Run*, Pink Floyd: *Dark Side of the Moon,* Fleetwood Mac: *Rumours.*
BACK COVER: (top) Led Zeppelin: *Led Zeppelin III*, Eagles: *Hotel California*, Original Soundtrack: *Saturday Night Fever* (bottom) Fleetwood Mac: *Rumours*, Pink Floyd: *Dark Side of the Moon*, Bruce Springsteen: *Born To Run*

Index